The GOD Room

by Danny Hahlbohm

The God Room
Copyright © 2014 Danny Hahlbohm
ISBN: 978-0-942507-23-2

All pieces of art in this book are original paintings by Danny Hahlbohm and they have all been
copyrighted in the name of Danny Hahlbohm.

Printed in the United States of America.
Published by:
Deeper Revelation Books
Revealing "the deep things of God" (1 Cor. 2:10)
P.O. Box 4260
Cleveland, TN 37320
423-478-2843
Website: www.deeperrevelationbooks.org
Email: info@deeperrevelationbooks.org

Many thanks to author Clay Harrison for permission
to use of his poem titled "Wings Of Faith" on page 107.

Unless otherwise noted, all Scripture quotations are from the
KING JAMES VERSION (KJV): public domain.

Scripture quotations marked (NLT) are taken from the
HOLY BIBLE, NEW LIVING TRANSLATION, copyright © 1996, 2004, 2007
by Tyndale House Foundation. Used by permission of Tyndale House Publishers Inc.,
Carol Stream, Illinois 60188. All rights reserved.

Scripture quotations marked (NIV) are taken from the
THE HOLY BIBLE, NEW INTERNATIONAL VERSION ®.
Copyright© 1973, 1978, 1984, 2011 by Biblica, Inc.TM.
Used by permission of Zondervan.

Scripture quotations marked (NKJV) are taken from the
NEW KING JAMES VERSION®. Copyright© 1982 by Thomas Nelson, Inc.
Used by permission. All rights reserved.

THE BRIDE OF CHRIST
Revelation 19:7-8

ACKNOWLEDGMENTS

I would like to first thank the Lord Himself for coming into my life and using me to be an instrument for His glory. Without His intervention, none of this could have ever been possible. Indeed, as the Bible clearly declares, Jesus Christ is the "Author and Finisher" (Hebrews 12:2).

I am forever grateful to "The Hound of Heaven" (the Holy Spirit) for tracking me down and, at times, dragging me while I clawed at the ground, into submission before the Lord. Without His relentless pursuit I am sure I would have never found my way home again.

A special appreciation and acknowledgement goes to my wife, Diana, for all her patience and endurance in living with an artist, a lifestyle that can, at times, be very challenging.

I would also like to thank all the many brothers and sisters in the Lord who have influenced my life, especially Pastor Jim MacInnes. I have spent many long hours drinking in his Spirit-filled messages which have helped me immensely and shaped my walk with the Lord. The flock needs a good shepherd.

I would also like to thank Mike Shreve, who "went the extra mile" and put in many long hours to make this book possible. Without his sincere dedication, this dream may have never become a reality. Throughout the production stage, Mike has become not only my publisher and chief editor, but a dear and close friend as well.

Finally, I would like to dedicate this book to you. It is for you that this book has been compiled. I pray that the Lord will open your heart to the ideas and stories God has given me. May they bring hope and encouragement to you. Other brothers and sisters have encouraged me greatly through the years and strengthened me on my journey. Now it is time for me to pass the blessings on. We are indeed a family, the family of God.

PREFACE

This book has been written to share with you the countless miracles, both physical and spiritual, that I have personally witnessed in my life and how the Lord has brought me through each of them, all for my benefit and growth. Although this book contains many actual events in my life, I do not share them to draw attention to myself, but that you can gain insight from what the Lord has shown me. What God has done for others He is willing to also do for you. God is not a respector of persons; we all are equal in His eyes. His gifts are given freely to anyone who will receive. All that is required is to say, "Yes Lord, here am I also. Use my life as You will."

No, I have not seen the seas parted, but I have seen the night sky open up in front of me. I have not witnessed many of the miracles God did in biblical times, but I have witnessed countless miracles that God has performed for me personally. He indeed is the same yesterday, today and tomorrow.

A famous quotation often used says, "Know thyself," but as children of the living God it is much more important to know who we are in Christ. Yes, I am an artist, chosen to spread His Word through art around the world, however, the work that I do is far more than that. My calling in life is to help heal those beaten down by the enemy, to encourage them through my art so these "soldiers of God" can regain their strength once again to fight the good fight for yet another day in His name.

I am not just an artist. I am a servant to the King. Be it art, music, or writing, I shall continue to serve Him until He deems it time for me to come home. At such time, hopefully, I shall hear the words I so long to hear which were spoken almost two thousand years ago by the Lord Jesus Christ.

Matthew 25:21
"Well done, thou good and faithful servant."

THE GOD ROOM

TABLE OF CONTENTS

> LION OF JUDAH
> Revelation 5:5

The EARLY Years

I suppose the best place to start is in the beginning. To do this truthfully, I need to begin even before I was born, when I was in my mother's womb.

My mom, Lois Lawrence Hahlbohm, was a Christian from early in her youth. She loved the Lord with all her heart and walked in the Lord as best she knew how. She was a firm believer in faith and prayers. Often she would speak to the Lord whenever she entered her own "God Room."

The God Room isn't necessarily a physical place, but rather, a spiritual place. In this spiritual sanctuary, you spend quiet alone time with the Lord just you and God. I suppose one could call it a "God Space," but I like to think of it as a gateway entrance, a portal into the presence of the Lord a place where you and God sit and talk.

Having accepted the Lord as our Savior and repenting of our sins, we become the son and daughters of God through Jesus Christ. Now we are invited into a place of intimacy with God.

Hebrews 4:16 NIV
"Let us then approach God's throne of grace with confidence, so that we may receive mercy and find grace to help us in our time of need."

UNKNOWN PATH
Psalm 32:7-8

This is our God Room. Whenever and wherever we spend quality alone time with the Lord in His presence, we are in the God Room, a place where the Bible proclaims that we can approach God's throne of grace with confidence.

Before the death of Christ, a high priest was the only one who was allowed to come before the Lord. Behind the long, thick veil, the priest would enter in and make the atonements and supplications for the people. Since the death and resurrection of our Lord Jesus Christ, born-again Christians have now become God's chosen priests. It is no longer necessary for us to make our requests known through another. We are now permitted and even invited to sit with Christ in heavenly places as a royal priesthood and rulers with the Lord.

1 Peter 2:9 NKJV
"But you are a chosen generation, a royal priesthood, a holy nation, His own special people, that you may proclaim the praises of Him who called you out of darkness into His marvelous light."

Ephesians 2:4-6 NKJV
"But God, who is rich in mercy, because of His great love with which He loved us, even when we were dead in trespasses, made us alive together with Christ (by grace), and raised us up together, and made us sit together in the heavenly places in Christ Jesus."

This is the premise of the God Room. Our quiet alone time, focused on heavenly things, we can actually commune with the Almighty God, separated from the world. Through Christ, we are provided a supernatural cloak of righteousness, not merely in the natural fine linen garments like the priests of old. We are baptized and cleansed through the Holy Spirit as we enter into the very throne room of God, the God Room.

When we set aside this special time for Him, with no computers, no TV, no conversation with others, no distractions of any kind, then we allow a spiritual opening to occur where we can stand before the King of kings Himself and bring our prayers directly to Him or to simply sit at His feet and hear His teachings and guidance.

My usual God Room is sitting on my back porch in the morning with a cup of coffee, talking with the Lord before I start my day. Sometimes I talk to the Lord about things; sometimes I just sit and listen to what He has to say, and sometimes we simply sit side by side and say nothing, just enjoying the sunrise, taking in God's magnificent handiwork in the heavens.

When I mention talking with God or times when God speaks to me, I do not mean an audible voice. Many times in God's Word we read of groups of people or individuals actually hearing the audible voice of God, but that is not what I am

Lois & Dick - Just Married

talking about. That does happen—but most of the time, God speaks to me within my spirit. At times, that inner voice seems so loud that it booms throughout my surroundings, but most of the time, it is that "still small voice" mentioned in a visitation that Elijah received from God (quoted below):

1 Kings 19:11-12
"And, behold, the Lord passed by, and a great and strong wind rent the mountains, and brake in pieces the rocks before the Lord; but the Lord was not in the wind: and after the wind an earthquake; but the Lord was not in the earthquake: And after the earthquake a fire; but the Lord was not in the fire: and after the fire a still small voice."

At times my God Room is in the car as I drive to some destination. Anywhere and anytime I set aside time to be alone with God without outside influences, that becomes my God Room, a portal by which I enter a realm of infinite possibilities, a place where transforming grace and miracle power can always be found. Such access is made possible by the Lord Jesus Christ Himself, "for through Him we both have access by one Spirit to the Father" (see Ephesians 2:18).

Often my mom would spend hours before the Lord in her God Room. She was almost eight months pregnant with me (her firstborn) when the first attack was made on my life. My dad and mom did not have any money. After the war, they were living in the basement of a friend's house until my dad found work.

One day while making her way down the long flight of steep stairs that led to the basement, Mom felt a push. In midflight, between the top of the stairs and the cement floor 10 feet below, she was caught up by an angel on her way into heaven.

She knew her life (and mine) had come to an end because she was being escorted into heaven's gates by this angel. She had no idea what was happening and did not understand such things. All she knew was that she felt she was on her way to paradise, and she was not ready to go just yet. She looked up and recited God's Word back to Him, "Lord, as Hannah gave Samuel to You, so do I give this child I carry to You also. If You will but grant my plea and allow me to deliver this child, I shall commit

RICHARD W. HAHLBOHM 1943

him to You to give You glory with all the gifts You may bestow" (see 1 Samuel 1:27).

By having received God's blessing upon her and her child, she felt herself being slowly returned to earth. My mom said she immediately was shot back into her body midflight above the stairs and gently floated like a feather onto the concrete floor. It all happened in super-slow-motion because of the angel holding her in his arms. She never received so much as a small bruise from the fall.

God had interceded on my mom's behalf, counteracting the enemy's push that placed her in such peril, almost costing both our lives. Mom told me many years later that she never forgot that day or the covenant she made with the Lord regarding me. I have no doubt that many times it was my mom's prayers that saved me, not only that day, but also in other life-threatening situations.

When my dad heard Mom's scream, he rushed quickly to her side. When Mom told him what had happened, he, too, began to thank the Lord for His mercy and grace, for my father was no stranger to the Lord. He had physically seen His glory years before on a battlefield. That story needs to be told.

At the age of seventeen, Richard W. Hahlbohm, had enlisted in the 101st Airborne Division during World War II. He was a paratrooper for the United States Army. In his first mission overseas, he was dropped into combat near Eerde, Holland, where he and the other troops made their way through thick forests during the night. My father witnessed a truly amazing, unforgettable spiritual incident. Here is the account in his own words:

Danny Hahlbohm - Age 5

"It all started about five o'clock in the morning after we dug in the thick forest. We had traveled for about one hour and the Germans were shelling the wooded area up ahead. It started to get heavier and heavier, coming toward us. The worst kind of shelling was the "tree bursts" because it threw shrapnel in all directions, and the trees would explode around us. At this time, we were told to move out into a clearing about three hundred yards to our left. We dug ourselves in, making trenches and foxholes, still hearing the shelling move by us and into the woods.

Suddenly, we began to hear small arms fire from the enemy advancing on both sides of us. We hunkered down in our holes to avoid being seen. All of a sudden, it got quiet. I heard one of my buddies call my name. I put my bayonet on my rifle, figuring we were being attacked. He called once again and told me to look to my left. I slowly raised my head above the foxhole and saw something that gave me chills all over. There was a bright white cloud, like a fog or mist, shaped like a man! As it started to rise, it became clearer and clearer. One by one, we began to get out of our foxholes, standing there in complete awe and falling to our knees. It was then I was able to make out the form; it was our Lord Jesus Christ!

He was floating in the air looking down on us. His hands and arms were outstretched in a three-quarter downward hold. I can't explain the feeling of peace and humbleness we all had. The stillness was such as I had never experienced before. The shelling had stopped, as did the small arms fire. All was quiet and peaceful. Then as quick as it all appeared, the mist of Jesus evaporated. The rest of the company had fallen back into the woods. We were the only section of the company who had witnessed this event. We talked about it amongst ourselves and decided not to mention it because we would all seem to be insane. I had thought of this many times and still wondered why we were all spared from death that day. It brought me closer to God, even in the midst of battle."

On December 19, 1944, my father was captured by the Germans in the bloody battle at Bastongne, the well-known "Battle of the Bulge." The Germans took the captive

American's boots and forced them to walk through the snow miles away to Stalag 4B. My father lost two of his toes due to frostbite during that march and had to have them cut off with a paring knife. He never forgot that miraculous night of seeing Jesus in a cloud above him. He was reassured that God was with him and kept him alive during his incarceration as a prisoner of war.

When the war was over, my father returned home to the United States. He was a decorated hero with many ribbons of honor, including the Bronze Star, Purple Heart, Belgian Croix De Gueerre, French Croix De Guerre, and fourteen other medals and commemorative decorations he earned.

My mom gave birth to their first child, Danny Richard Hahlbohm, in Mineola, Long Island, New York, on June 22, 1949, at five o'clock in the morning. I weighed less than five pounds and needed extra care and feeding to gain the strength I needed to survive. I was allergic to milk and other substitutes, which was a serious concern. Soon, I began running a 105 degree fever and turning blue. The doctors ran tests and told my mother my stomach was upside down and I needed an operation immediately. My condition was critical, and due to my frailness, the chance of making it through this operation was very slim.

My mother truly believed that outside forces were once again trying to take her child. However, she had faith in God that He would not let this happen, especially since she had a covenant with the Lord regarding my life. She once again got alone with the Lord and began to pray, asking God to intervene, trusting in His mercy and grace, and holding fast to His Word. She felt the Lord's assurance that He had not forgotten their covenant, and He told her to seek another doctor's opinion.

DAD AS COXSACKIE COP 1959

When she went to another doctor, he told her my condition was merely a lack of calcium not an upside-down stomach. He also gave her instructions to boil skim milk for my feeding. It worked! The fever broke and I began to gain weight.

Soon I was a healthy baby boy again because my mother kept her faith in God, trusted in His Word, and made time to seek the Lord each day. Her personal time alone with God became even more important as time went on. I am sure that pillar of faith and her continuous prayers in her God Room, thwarted the Enemy's attack on me throughout the years, even after she passed away. God never forgets His promises to those who serve and follow Him.

Numbers 23:19

"God is not a man, that he should lie; neither the son of man, that he should repent: hath he said, and shall he not do it? or hath he spoken, and shall he not make it good?"

I really had a wonderful childhood. To this day, I consider those years to be the happiest days of my life. We lived in a small house in Hicksville, Long Island, New York. In 1957, at the age of eight, we moved to upstate New York to a small town on the Hudson River called Coxsackie, about nineteen miles south of Albany. I was sad to leave all my friends in Hicksville, but I was also excited about living in the country. Within the first few weeks, I explored the basement of this small two-bedroom house. The previous owners had swept all the dirt and debris into one large pile in the middle of the concrete basement floor.

I started to rummage through it and came across a small, paperback book. As I brushed the dirt aside, I became fascinated by the beautiful lines and curves the artist had created. It was my first real look at art for the sake of art. This artist was a master at his craft. There was just one small problem in all this appreciation: It was a Playboy paperback book with drawings of women in negligees.

As a young boy of eight, the anatomy and sexual content eluded me. Instead, I was fascinated by the artwork. I was young, naive, innocent and failed to see past the artistic stokes. However, the Enemy (Satan) knew full well the trap he had set before me and figured if he could not kill me (as he had tried many times before), he would corrupt the gift the Lord has graciously given to me.

I grabbed a piece of paper and a pencil and proceeded to imitate these lines myself. I became ecstatic to find that I could draw the lines with the same accuracy as this artist. I was so proud and I wanted to show the world. Even though I may not have understood the anatomy, I was old enough to know from that still small voice inside, not to show the drawings to my parents, if I wanted to live to tell about it. So I decided I

would do the next best thing.

I had met some boys in the neighborhood, ages fourteen to sixteen years old, that I could show my drawings to. Not only would they compliment me on my work, but perhaps I could impress them enough to become "one of the boys." They liked the drawings alright, but they laughed at me when I told them I drew them. No one believed me, no one. The only ones who might have believed me were my parents, but that was too risky indeed. I ripped them up, but I was still so proud I could do what this famous artist did. No one knew about my artistic gift, but I knew . . . I knew.

God had indeed given me a special gift and the Enemy was already at work to corrupt it. Perhaps Satan's ploy would have worked, but the Lord provided another deterrent that no little boy could resist, a puppy.

My father was a town cop (one of three) and gained much respect in the small community. One day, he gave me what every young boy dreams of: his very own dog, a German Shepherd! His name was King. We immediately became the very best of friends and I never went anywhere, except to school, without King. We would venture out into the woods that surrounded my house and spend hours just roaming the countryside. He was as curious as I was about everything.

As we both grew older, we also grew closer. My mom's frequent times alone with the Lord and God answering her prayers counteracted the Enemy's move. The battle was to be the Lord's. I often wondered if there was more to my dog King than met the eye. There is no limitation to God's love and grace in our lives.

Not too far from my house in the country was a small patch of grass along the roadside that the county mowed frequently. It sloped upward into the woods behind it. Occasionally, I would go there to lie back and look at the clouds as they rolled by. One day as I lay there, turning clouds into sheep and dragons, I fell asleep with King at my side as always. I remember being awakened by a muffled growling close to my head. As I slowly opened my eyes, I heard a horrible hissing noise getting louder and more ferocious. Still lying there, I tilted my head backward to where the sound was coming from. There, upside down in my eyesight, inches away from my face, was the biggest and muskrat I had ever seen!

Looking backward into the eyes of death, I became paralyzed lying there on the ground with my neck fully exposed to this creature. I remember seeing this monster's eyes suddenly open wider as it began to lunge for my throat, almost as if it were in slow motion. Frozen in utter terror and unable to move a muscle, I lay there almost beckoning the creature's advance.

Out of nowhere, a big swoosh came across me and the monster was gone. King, my faithful bodyguard and friend, snatched the creature out in midair just as it lunged. The fight took place only three or four feet from me. Blood and fur were flying in all directions. King attacked with such a vengeance, I was glad that he was on my side. Within minutes, the fight was over and the monster lay dead with its large fangs still open and its tongue hanging out. King came

to me to make sure I was okay and licked me all over. Still in shock over the whole ordeal, I hugged my heaven sent bodyguard just as tightly as I could.

The muskrat was so huge I could barely drag it back to the house a quarter of a mile away. But I had to show everyone how King had saved me. As I dragged this beast to the

DICK AND KING AT HUDSON RIVER

house by its huge leathery tail, King kept nipping at it, making sure it was dead. I appreciated that factor. When I finally got home and showed it to my father, he could not believe its size. They took pictures of the muskrat and presented it to the newspaper in town. We were told that it was the largest one of its kind in that county. My father was so glad I was okay, and he was also proud of King and bought him the biggest steak in the

general store! King was definitely King that day!

I never looked at King the same way again. Before that day, King was just my friend, my buddy I loved very much and knew that he loved me. Now, King was my protector with a vicious side to anything that would do me harm. It felt good and scary at the same time. In hindsight, I know it was another confirmation of the covenant between my mom and God many years ago. I often wondered if God had sent some angels there to help King in this victory over such a large beast. All I knew was that I was glad King and God were on my side and that I had a woman of God for a mother who never forgot to mention me in her daily visits to her God Room. I would be even more aware of this fact as time went on.

My father bought an outboard motorboat. We would ski behind this boat down the Hudson River, before it became too polluted to do so. My father would drop the boat in the water at the boat ramp a half mile away and then cruise in the boat to pick me up on the rocky riverbank just a few hundred yards from our house. I would climb onboard, and we would be off for a day of skiing.

One sunny day as I skipped over the rocks to greet my father on the riverbank, suddenly, he shouted, "STOP! Don't move a muscle!" My foot was suspended in midair over the next rock. As I looked down, I saw a nest of water moccasins just beneath my foot.

"Just move back slowly," my father said. "Really slow."

As I started to back away, I could see all the snakes that were sunning on the rocks, coiled back and ready to strike. A water moccasin is one of the most deadly snakes in North America. Once again, God's protection was covering me as King came rushing in, making short work of all the snakes. There were approximately four to five nests in that immediate area, maybe nine to twelve snakes in all. Fortunately, and quite remarkably, King was never bitten. Yes, King received another prime steak for his efforts, but my mom gave all the glory to the Lord.

Luke 10:19

"Behold, I give unto you power to tread on serpents and scorpions, and over all the power of the enemy: and nothing shall by any means hurt you."

In later years, when both my mom and I were much older, I remember her telling me there were many times when the Lord would bring me to her attention, and allow her to sense traps that lay before me I never saw. She would go to her God Room or someplace where she could spend time alone with the Lord and pray for me, not leaving until she had assurance all was well again.

We often wonder how many well-laid traps the Enemy has set before us that God has thwarted and destroyed. These are things that go totally unnoticed by us and shall remain unknown until we are with the Lord and He opens the book to show us all the times He has protected us from traps unaware.

Not long ago I was watching a TV broadcast where a minister opened his sermon by looking directly at his congregation and asked them, "Do you think you are sitting here merely by accident? I declare to you today that you are here as a child of God, sitting in His house because someone, somewhere, prayed for you prior to today."

I tend to agree with him 100 percent. Our prayers for loved ones and family members allow the many blessings God bestows on all of us. We are showered with countless blessings every day, all day long. We need to pray one for another as commanded by Jesus so we can send countless showers of blessings to flow from heaven's gate onto our loved ones, protecting them from harm, seen or unseen.

To receive these blessings, we must be in the right place to be given that flow from heaven and remain close the Lord, becoming more like Him by spending quality alone time in the God Room.

PRAYER WARRIOR
1 John 5:14-15

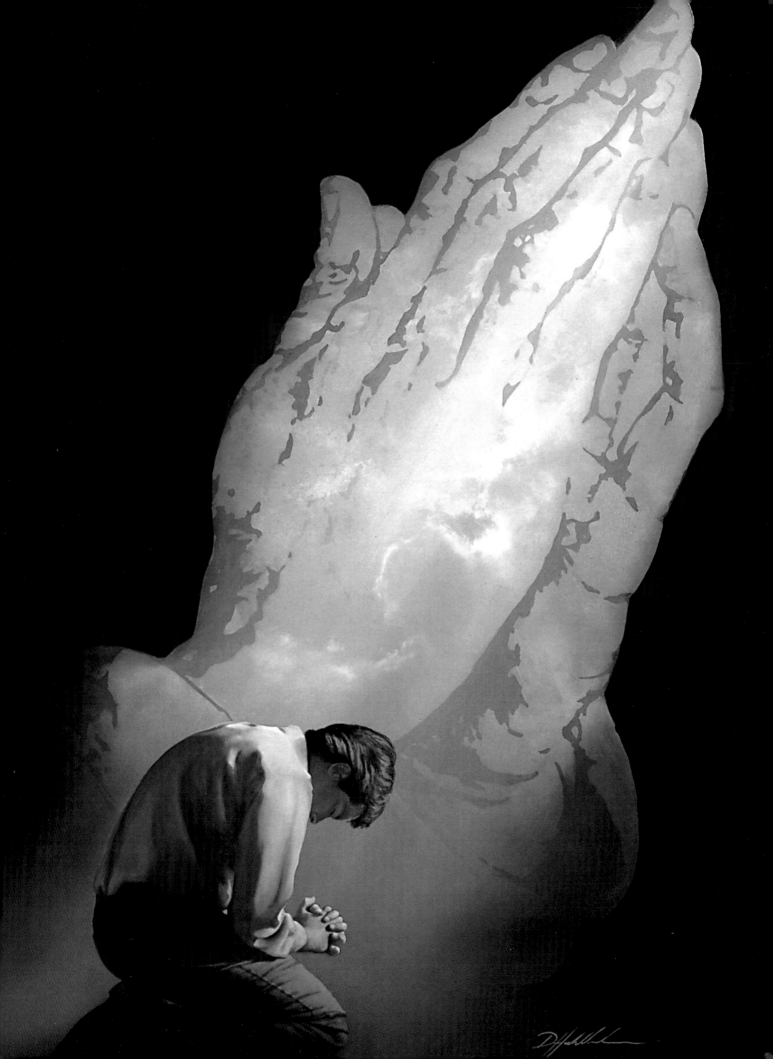

2
The DARK Waters

Shortly afterward, we moved back to Long Island, New York, to another small town in Lake Panamoka. It was about an hour and a half east of New York City. I was excited because I was going to be close to my cousin, Albert. We were like brothers whenever we were together. Albert was adopted by Grandma, which made him more my uncle than cousin, but since we were only a year apart, everyone considered us cousins.

Within months of moving to Long Island, my mom began seeing her sister on a regular basis. Unfortunately during this time, my mom got involved with the Ouija Board tarot reading. She began spending more time with these than she spent time with the Lord, so during this time span, I began getting into serious trouble with the law.

Sometimes in our Christian walk we lose out footing, but we must always be aware that there is a spiritual war going on, even if we do not see or hear the bullets passing close by our heads. It is imperative that we lean on the Word of God and seek Him each day on a regular basis. The Enemy never sleeps and is constantly pushing against the door to find a way in. Even the tiniest crack is enough for an evil force to gain access by prying the door open for more like himself.

I AM THE LIGHT
Psalm 27:1

My grandma was diagnosed with cancer and everyone knew she did not have long to live. On one usual weekly trip over to my Aunt Lorrena's house, my mom began playing with the Ouija Board. After a few minutes, they allowed me to ask it a question? I asked when Grandma was going to die.

The glass spun around and spelled out FEB172AM, February 17 at two o'clock in the morning. I did not really believe in such things, but I thought to myself, If Grandma does die at that time and date, then the board had to be true. Right?

Several months went by and we almost forgot about the prediction made at my aunt's house. One morning as I was getting ready for school, I came into the living room to say goodbye to my mom. I noticed she and Dad were sitting at the coffee table unusually silent and sad. My mom said, "Danny, last night your Grandma passed away. I'm sorry, son, but she is gone."

"When did she die?" my dad asked.

"Oh, last night in the middle of the night. I was by her side when she died, around 2 a.m. I think."

It took me a couple of minutes and then I remembered. "What? 2 a.m.? What day is this? Don't you remember? That is what the Ouija Board said, February 17 at 2 o'clock in the morning!" We just stared at each other for a few moments with our jaws on the floor.

How completely different and at opposite ends of the spectrum God and Satan go about recruiting new converts and believers to their side of the "fence." God says, "Have faith first and I will show you miracles beyond comprehension." Satan says, "You need not have faith at all to join me. I show mysterious things to even the most skeptical."

One is a trap meant to hold you captive; the other breaks all bonds to set you free. With each trick, the devil is providing crumbs for us to follow the path that eventually leads down a dark corridor and into the hidden cage at the end. I had just swallowed my first crumb from Satan's hand, and without prayers (which had protected me thus far), I had little chance of escape without God's intervention.

Both Albert and I continued to hang out with the wrong crowd and got deeper and deeper into trouble with the law. Finally, our run-ins with the law became so great that just days before Albert was to appear in court and be locked-up for violating his probation, he jumped on his motorcycle, waved goodbye, and that was the last time I saw Albert until after the war.

In 1968 the Vietnam War was raging. I enlisted in the Air Force and became a radar technician on the Phantom F-4s. They shipped me to Vietnam. Thank God that by

DANNY IN BOOT CAMP 1968

this time, my mom had come back to the Lord, and, once again, I was in her prayers. I am sure those long heartfelt prayers kept many a stray bullet from finding its mark. It is so good to be in the hands of God.

The last year of my enlistment as the war came to a close, they sent me to England to serve the rest of my term. I was thinking to myself, *It will be easy living from here on out with the war behind me now.* Little did I know that in peaceful merry-ole England I was to have the biggest battle of my life, and I was not prepared. The war I encountered was a war from within, and more was at stake than just my life; my very soul was threatened!

In 1971 I arrived at Bentwaters England AFB to serve out the rest of my military tour. A group of us formed a band to pass the time. We practiced almost every night at the lead guitar's house, which was off base. The practices were usually two or three hours long. Afterwards, we'd just hang around for a while before heading back to base. During one of our breaks, I mentioned my experience regarding my grandmother and the foretelling of the Ouija Board. Everyone got excited. After that we formed a habit each night after band practice playing the Ouija Board.

It didn't take long before we escalated to doing séances, of which I became the medium. Before long, we were captive audiences to many strange happenings. More foretold happenings came to past; objects moved in the room; and supernatural strength was revealed through me as a spirit entered into my being. The devil's trap had been set, and we all took it "hook, line, and sinker."

This continued for several months until the band broke up and we had no place to hold the séances. When another buddy heard what we were doing, he said we could use his room on base to hold the séances. His roommate insisted on being a part of the séances as well.

When we agreed for the roommate to be included, we didn't know he had a hidden secret. Soon we realized that something else was going on. As it turned out, this roommate was practiced in what he called Transcendental Meditation, another tool of the occult. During the séances,

DANNY AFTER THE WAR 1972

he was using this tool against me and the spirits that had entered me. An evil spiritual clash occurred that nearly cost both of us our lives.

We began as usual, with the reading of the Bible. We foolishly thought reading the Bible would protect us from evil spirits; thereby, allowing only good spirits to come in. When we turned off the lights, immediately I could see a strange glow around the roommate. Instantly, a powerful spirit entered me, and I tried to clear my

mind of it as I had done many times in the past. This time I could not. Realizing I was powerless and at the mercy of this entity, I could feel every aspect of its rage.

Terror gripped me as I began to see a swarm of tiny demons, maybe one- to two-feet in stature, come from behind and from within me, encircling the roommate. There must have been at least eighty to one hundred of them possessing me. I could feel the insane rage and thoughts this evil spirit possessed. Having this connection, I knew the demons wanted to destroy the other spirit inside the roommate by taking my hands, plunging them deep into his chest, ripping it open, and killing him. As I lunged forward, a super bright light flashed, lighting up the entire room. We collided in midair and fell hard to the ground.

Needless to say, that was the last séance I ever held. However, during the weeks afterward, I began suffering severe migraine headaches to the point of losing my vision and blacking out. At times the pain was unbearable. I was eating aspirin like they were candy, but without relief. I decided to see the local psychiatrist, but he could not see me for a minimum of a few weeks. I made an appointment, but I knew I was not going to last long. I was right.

The pain increased and by the third day, it all came to a head while I was in the barracks. Hopping out of bed, I thought perhaps fresh air would relieve some of the pressure and pain. As I walked down the long hallway to the door, I remember passing other guys in the hall and hearing their voices, but I never saw one person, only white around me. Reaching the end of the hall, I pushed the door open.

It was late October in the northern part of England and a thick fog, thicker than I had ever seen, had rolled in that night. I stood outside for a while trying to breathe some fresh air, hoping to clear my head of the pressure and pain, but all I got was the cold, freezing wetness of the fog that drove me back inside. I have no memory of how many times I repeated this routine. Finally, I ran across the grounds a few hundred yards and dropped to my knees feeling like death was upon me.

The fog was so thick, I could barely see ten feet in front of me. There were trees on the grounds, but I could not see any of them. As I knelt there, dying from the crushing pressure and pain, I made a final plea for God to save my life. Looking toward heaven, I cried out in pure desperation, "God, I don't know if You are real or not, but this thing is taking my life! If You are there; if You are real, please, God, help me!"

Soaked to the bone from the cold, thick fog that enveloped me, I pleaded for my life. At once, I saw the fog open up with a tunnel leading straight into the heavens! As I gazed upward through the three- or four-feet wide tunnel. I still could not see anything but fog. Then I felt God remove the crushing pressure and pain from me like it was a mere speck of lint on my shoulder. It was almost as if God was saying, "Oh, is this what is troubling you? There, how's that?" Instantly, it was gone!

I made my way back to the barracks, shivering and cold from the wet fog that had drenched me to the bone. In my mind I kept repeating to myself, I saw God! I came face to face with God! There IS a God; I just met Him! I MET GOD!

I needed to know more about this Supreme Being. I honestly didn't know if this was God, Buddha, Jesus, or whoever, but I knew there was indeed a Supreme Being, and He had saved my life. I wanted to know who He was.

Two months later, I was honorably discharged from the service. I went home to my parents who now lived in Woodbine, New Jersey, and began my quest in finding out who that Supreme Being was. I asked my parents, their ministers, other ministers, Catholics, Protestants, Jews, Hindus, and everyone I could think of. They all had their own take on the subject, but I was looking for something different, something more dramatic or perhaps more complicated. Either way, I was looking for a sign rather than being led by the Spirit. How funny it is that sometimes the very thing we are looking for is right in front of our face, but we just do not see it. In the Gospels, Jesus often taught about letting those who have eyes see and those who have ears hear (see Mark 4:23). I was trying to come to God on my own, not letting God (in His time) come to me.

I decided to buy a Bible and find the answers for myself, but every time I opened the Bible to read a few lines, I would stop and wonder what I had just read. It made no sense to me at all. Over and over, I would read a passage or two without any idea of what the scripture meant. Eventually, I gave up and decided I would know when I know and went about my way.

Even though I had the hunger, God's timing was not right just yet. The Lord had one particular person in mind who would lead me to Him, someone I trusted dearly. This was someone with whom I had grown up with and shared my deepest, darkest secrets. The Lord was preparing this person who was willing to travel thousands of miles to share the Word of God with me. He was on his way.

How great is that? That we serve a loving and giving God which not only directs our path in order to find His grace but provides other people to travel long distances in bringing that good news to us. What a precious and wonderful God we serve.

John 6:65
"Therefore said I unto you, that no man can come unto me, except it were given unto him of my Father."

NOT ALONE
Joshua 1:9

THE DARK WATERS

3
Into
THE LIGHT

I received word that my cousin Albert was coming from California. I had not heard from Albert for five years. The last I saw him, he hopped on his bike and headed to California, fleeing from the law. Now I heard rumors that he was married and had become a priest! Married? Perhaps, but a priest? I don't think so!

I headed for Aunt Mickey's house in Riverhead, New York, to meet Al and his new wife. When Albert came up the driveway, I could not believe my eyes. He had not changed one bit. He looked the same as I remembered him five years earlier. We embraced each other with a bear hug that I thought was going to kill us both. He whispered in my ear as we embraced, "Danny, I need to speak to you alone as soon as possible." There was something in the way he said that. Albert looked the same but inside, something was different.

The whole family greeted each other, meeting his new wife and trying to catch up on the past few years. When the conversation died down a bit, Albert once again turned to me and said, "Danny, let's go some place where we can talk alone." I pointed out to the cemetery across the street, we hopped over the fence and sat down, leaning against some tombstones. Who would have guessed that among the dead, I would find life?

> ### HE IS RISEN
> John 1:14

Al told me about how he became a born-again Christian and that the Lord told him to fly to New York just to tell me about Jesus. He explained how the Lord literally put $2,000 in his pockets when he did his laundry, emptying his pockets beforehand. He and his wife were living in poverty level at the time, and could never have made the trip otherwise. Most of all, he wanted to tell me how Christ had died and risen again for anyone who would accept Him and believe on Him as the Son of God. I clung to every word as if it were pure gold, not simply because it was Al who was telling me this, but because deep in my heart, I knew this was truth!

In my desperate search for God months before, I had heard about Jesus being the Son of the Living God, how He died on the cross and was resurrected. The difference now was I felt that the Holy Spirit sitting beside us in that cemetery among the dead, anointing each word Albert spoke to me about Christ. It was not just the fact that I grew up with Al and trusted him to tell me the truth. If that were the case, I would have listened to what he said, maybe raised an eyebrow and told him, "Hmm. I'll give it some thought." However, I knew that this was the truth and not coming from the lips of a person, but rather from the witness of the Holy Spirit. God had now come to me, not me seeking to come to Him.

INTO THE LIGHT

John 15:16
"Ye have not chosen me, but I have chosen you."

I began to tell Al about my experience in England and how God had saved my life, leaving out none of the details. Albert had tears streaming down his face as he lifted his hands high and began to praise God! Then he said a few sentences in a strange language I had never heard and embraced me once again. "God is so good!" he said, "I knew this was a mighty calling I had to follow."

Albert continued to tell me about Jesus and being saved. When he finished, he asked me if I wanted to accept Christ there with him. I told him I wanted to, but I felt it was something I needed to do in private. We prayed together and left the graveyard to join the rest of the family in the house.

Later that evening, after we retired to our rooms, I told Albert I had given it much thought and was going to accept Jesus into my heart that night. He told me if I needed him, he was next door. I went to my room, knelt by the bed, and began to pray.

No sooner had I begun then I found my mind wandering, thinking of everything but what I wanted to pray about. I stopped, opened my eyes, cleared my head, and tried my prayer a second time. Again, hundreds of thoughts came rushing to my mind. Thoughts of what I did last week, what I was wearing, what my father told me years ago, the bills I had to pay, and the horror of Vietnam all came rushing in at once. My mind was jammed with total confusion and chaos. It was like a hundred projectors overlapping each other in video and audio were projecting on one small screen.

I knocked on Albert's door and told him what was happening. He frowned a bit and said he understood. Then he told me that Satan, the author of confusion, was interfering with my acceptance of Christ. He told me he and his wife would be praying for me and rebuking the devil.

Again, I experienced the same confusion. I tried one more time with all my heart and accepted Jesus Christ as my Lord and Savior. As soon as my prayer was completed, I felt someone touch my forehead with a finger. I figured it was Albert, but when I opened my eyes, I found that no one was there. The door was still closed. I thought I had just imagined it, but it was so real. I really did feel someone touch me.

The next morning at breakfast, I told Albert I had accepted Jesus and he praised God at the top of his lungs there in front of everyone. I told him about the finger touching my forehead and he said he wasn't sure, but in Revelations 14:1 it says when we accept Christ, a new name is written on our foreheads. Perhaps, it was an angel or the Lord Himself. All I know is that I had not imagined it. I felt it as clearly as day. Sometimes, I can still feel a touch in the exact spot on my forehead, like there truly is some kind of impression left there.

Albert immediately told me the very first thing I must do is to dig into the Word of God, explaining, "Just like we need food to sustain our bodies, we also need spiritual food (the Bible) to maintain our spiritual health."

Matthew 13:4
"And when he sowed, some seeds fell by the way side, and the fowls came and devoured them up."

ONE SOLITARY LIFE
1 Corinthians 3:13

INTO THE LIGHT

He never wrote a book. He never held
an office. He never had a family or owned
a home. He didn't go to college. He never
lived in a big city. He never traveled 200
miles from the place where he was born.
He did none of the things that usually
accompany greatness. He had no credentials
but himself.

He was only 33 when the tide of public opinion
turned against him. His friends ran away. One
of them denied him. He was turned over to his
enemies and went through the mockery of a trial.
He was nailed to a cross between two thieves.
While he was dying, his executioners gambled
for his garments, the only property he had on earth.
When he was dead, he was laid in a borrowed grave,
through the pity of a friend.

Twenty centuries have come and gone, and today
he is the central figure of the human race.
All the armies that ever marched,
all the navies that ever sailed,
all the parliaments that ever sat,
all the kings that ever reigned--
put together--have not affected the
life of man on this earth as much as that

one solitary life.

Immediately, I opened my Bible and started reading. I read about three paragraphs and stopped. My mouth dropped open and I understood. Here was another wonderful miracle of God right before my eyes. I now understood what I was reading from the Bible!

If I had read those verses months ago, I could not have understood the passage. It would be like reading Greek. Now, without any literary changes or teaching, I was able to understand what I was reading. With the help of the Holy Spirit, I was able to understand it all! In one night, my comprehension changed. Like a blind and deaf man before the Lord, I could now understand and hear from God.

Albert died a couple years later in an accident on his bike in California. Whatever my life has been, if I have helped or encouraged others in any way concerning their walk with God, it is because Albert was a faithful servant to the Lord and traveled thousands of miles just to tell me about Jesus. If I receive any rewards for good things I have done in this life on earth, then indeed a portion of those rewards belong to Albert as well. Thank you, brother.

Soon after I married, we purchased a small house in North Bellport, Long Island, New York. I was working part time for an art gallery, but I managed to do my first painting of Christ. It was titled "One Solitary Life", a thirty-six-inch by forty-eight-inch painting that hung in the middle of our living room, along with other pictures and shelves.

One night around two o'clock in the morning, my wife began shaking me abruptly screaming, "THE HOUSE IS ON FIRE!" I awoke to find flames coming out of the small closet where the boiler tank was located. Smoke was everywhere. We managed to escape into the cold night and stood by the side of the road in the snow, watching our house burn to the ground.

After the firemen put the fire out, I saw another miracle from the hand of God. All that remained of the burned house was a small portion of the center wall in the living room. Hanging on that wall was the painting "One Solitary Life" without a scratch or burn anywhere! Even the fire hoses that put out the fire had not damaged that painting one inch. The edges of the painting were not touched by the flames that destroyed everything around it. The only thing that crossed my mind was a poem written many years ago by John Piper which said,

Only one life, 'twill soon be past;
Only what's done for Christ will last.

I was doing some paintings for a small local gallery in town, but it wasn't steady work, so I ended up working for my father-in-law at a farm and garden center forty-five minutes away. I continued to read God's Word each day as Albert had suggested. I also had time to enter into my quiet time alone with God on my way to and from work each day. I began to look forward to the long trip daily to be with the Lord. My car became my "God Room" with just me and God. We talked about many things traveling down the highway.

While driving home from work one day, enjoying my traveling God Room with the Lord, I began to feel an overwhelming presence of love from the Holy Spirit engulfing me completely. My eyes welled up as I scooted down the highway thanking the Lord for all He had done in my life and for loving me so. By the end of my 45-minute trip, basking in the love of God, I became a crying, sobbing puddle of mush. I pulled into the driveway, went straight downstairs (where I was doing some paintings), fell on my knees with tears streaming down my face and cried out, "Lord! You are so wonderful! Praise Your holy name, Father! Lord, you have given me so much. Let me give something back to You. Let me try to bless You in some way because of the way you have blessed me, O Lord!"

I felt a voice inside say, "Use the talent I have given you, My child."

Still looking up, I asked, "What would You have me to do, Lord?" There was no answer, but I felt an uncontrollable urge to put up a blank canvas and begin painting. My hands were busy mixing colors and applying them to the canvas with definitive strokes, yet I had no idea what I was painting. With no concept in mind, it was almost like I was painting blind. After an hour or so of painting, I stepped back and there on the canvas was an open sky with sunrays shining brightly through dark clouds. It captured my heart, but I knew it was not finished. Like a young excited child, I asked, "OK, Lord, now what's next?" No answer. As quickly as the inspiration came, it left. I knew the painting was not complete. There was nothing there but this powerful, dramatic sky and I had no idea how God wanted me to complete it. I put the brushes down, turned out the light, and went upstairs.

SECOND COMING
Matthew 24:27

As the days went by, each day I would go downstairs after work to paint the other paintings I had to do for the art shows, but still I had no inspiration to complete what God had started. I waited upon the Lord.

Two weeks later, I went downstairs as usual to paint, and I felt the Holy Spirit once again come over me. I grabbed the canvas, put it on the easel, stood back, and my mouth dropped to the floor! As I looked at the opening sky, then I also saw the face of Jesus as clearly as if it were projected on the canvas for me. It was not yet painted on the canvas, but all I had to do was fill in the areas with paint as I saw it.

Throughout the next couple of months, the Lord showed me how anything (even a simple painting) can be a powerful tool if given completely to the Lord. I proudly hung it up in our entryway for everyone to see what God had done, but I had no idea what He was about to do with this painting. It still astounds me to this day.

During this time, a close neighbor of ours, Phyllis, was coming over on a regular basis for coffee and conversation. She and her husband attended a local church and knew the teachings of the Bible, but they never knew Christ in a personal way. Often she would pass by the new painting hanging on the wall and remark, "Something about that painting gives me chills." Phyllis said she could never quite put her finger on it, but there was something about the painting that made her feel uncomfortable. She expressed that feeling almost every time she walked by it.

A few weeks later, she mentioned that she and Ed were going to take a short vacation upstate New York and asked if we would watch their house while they were away. We agreed. The following week, Phyllis and Ed returned and called, all excited. She said she wanted to come over to tell us about their trip.

She came in, bursting with joy, explaining that while they were up in New York with another couple, both she and Ed had accepted the Lord Jesus Christ as their personal Savior and had become born again Christians. We all hugged and rejoiced with her. On her way out the door, Phyllis once again glanced at the painting on the wall and said, "You know, I just love that painting, Danny."

I jumped up out of the chair, grabbed her arm, and said, "What?"

Phyllis turned around, startled for a moment and repeated, "I simply said that I love the new piece."

"Phyllis, don't you remember? You always hated that painting. You said it always gave you chills, as you put it."

Phyllis tilted her head, laid on finger to her cheek, and said, "Hmm . . . I don't know how I could have said that; it's wonderful!" Then she smiled and walked out the door.

To me, this was bona fide evidence that the Holy Spirit was working through this painting. Before Phyllis accepted the Lord, she was being convicted by the Holy Spirit and it left her feeling very uneasy. After becoming a born-again Christian, she was receiving warmth and joy from the same painting. Nothing changed but her heart and spirit. Now her spirit could rejoice with the Holy Spirit in something as simple as a painting. It was well with her soul.

God is a God of many miracles. He uses anything we give Him to perform those miracles, whether it be a loaf of bread and three fishes or a simple painting. As long as it is given to Him for His glory and purpose, God can perform many marvelous miracles in our lives through common, everyday things. He is just waiting for us to turn everything over to Him and simply believe. However, I did not know that God was not finished with the miracles He intended for this painting. I was soon to find out big time.

I applied for a local art show the following week and was accepted. My wife, Danise, was in her eighth month of pregnancy and we needed all the money we could come up with for this new addition. She was going to sit at the show while I went to work at the farm stand. I would relieve her in the evenings after I left work. Among the paintings was "The Second Coming." This was the first time it was publicly displayed outside our home. I prayed over the painting that it would bless the home of whomever purchased it.

When I returned to the show that evening, Danise said there had been a large number of people who showed interest in the painting, but no one purchased it. A few hours later, a young man asked about the painting. I briefly explained its history and told him the price. He told me it was quite reasonable, but he did not have the cash on him. He said he would return before the night was over with the money and asked if I could hold it for him until then. I explained that the weekends were our busiest times and that I could hold it until Friday evening at the very latest. Then it would go back up for sale if he had not returned with a deposit. He agreed but assured me he would be back for it either that night (Wednesday night) or the next morning at the latest.

The young man did not show up that night or the next morning as promised. By Friday evening, I told my wife to put the painting back up for sale. I had to do some small errands, so I left Danise to take care of the booth while I was away for an hour or so. When I returned, there was a crowd of people around the booth, security guards and all. Danise was crying hysterically. I pushed my way through the crowd and asked her what was the matter.

She said a woman came by right after I left and asked about the painting. She wrote a check, took the painting and left. Minutes later, the same guy who had wanted the painting Wednesday, came to the booth with a couple of buddies to show them the painting. When he found out that it was already sold, she said his face changed from a smile to utter hatred. Danise tried to explain that we held the painting as long as we could, just as we had agreed, but the young man would have none of it. He began yelling and screaming obscenities, cursing at my wife, and exclaiming that he wished her baby dead! Then he and his buddies were escorted out the door by security. She said it was as if he was demon possessed.

After the show that night, the phone rang when we got home. It was the lady who just bought the painting.

"Is this Mr. Hahlbohm?" she asked.

"Yes."

"Hi, I'm the woman who bought your painting today, "The Second Coming."

"Oh, yes. Are you enjoying it?"

"Well, that's what I'm calling about. You see, I brought the painting home and I hung it on the wall. When my husband came in, he was furious and told me I had to return it immediately. Would that be okay? I am sorry."

I told her it was fine, that I painted that piece to glorify the Lord and to be a blessing in someone's home, not to be a point of confrontation. She was relieved and said she would return it the first thing in the morning.

The next morning when I arrived at the show, she was there with the painting in hand. I gave back her check; she apologized again and left. As I hung the painting back up on the display rack, I heard the Lord say, "Don't sell it."

The voice was so clear that I spun around, looked up, and said, "What?" I heard the voice again inside my heart say, "Don't sell the painting." My heart fell to the floor. This was the one piece that seemed to be getting all the attention, and now I was not to sell it? We really needed every penny to make ends meet and to support the baby that was due the next month.

"Why?" I began pleading with God, explaining my position as if He didn't already know. But His answer was firm and consistent, "Do not sell the painting." I submitted to His will and took the price tag off the painting.

I told my wife that the painting was not for sale and explained what the Lord had said, but she did not buy any of it. Soon, the place was swarming with customers, asking about the painting. I had to tell them repeatedly that the painting was not for sale. I thought it best not to tell them, "God told me so," because most would either not believe me or suggest that I be committed to an asylum of some kind.

Some people even got irate and said "Well, then why do you have it on display if it is not for sale?" This went on all day, almost like a feeding frenzy. I had people actually pulling cash out of their pockets to coax me into selling the painting. All the while, I could see my wife in the background frowning. She did not understand either. God had not told her; He told me alone.

Finally, I broke away, got somewhere alone, cleared my mind, and entered into my God Room, making a final plea to God on His throne room floor.

The Lord said, "Be of good cheer. You have been obedient to My command and have not given into the temptation set before you. You asked for the painting to bless someone's home, and your intentions were pure, indeed, My child, but I have a better plan. Instead of blessing just one home with this painting, why not bless thousands? We shall make reproductions of this piece; thereby, spreading the blessings to many instead of just one."

I became excited, but then my heart sank as reality set in and I timidly added, "But Lord, it costs hundreds of dollars, if not thousands, to do that. I don't have that kind of money!"

All I heard back was as a simple soft response, "Have faith."

Now I was totally confused. I went back to the show, trying to figure out how I could come up with the money. As I was pondering this, a gentleman came up and asked once again about the painting. I told him it was not for sale, but as the light bulb turned on in my head, I replied, "There will be prints available." Without hesitating, the man reached into his pocket and asked how much of a deposit was needed to hold a print for him? God made a way!

I instructed my wife to begin taking names and deposits from anyone interested in purchasing prints of this painting. By the end of the show we had the funds to reproduce it.

Psalms 34:8
"O taste and see that the Lord is good: blessed is the man that trusteth in him."
Isaiah 22:22
"And the key of the house of David will I lay upon his shoulder; so he shall open, and none shall shut; and he shall shut, and none shall open."

The painting was not to be sold. The Lord shut the door that no one could open, not even those who purchased it and placed it in their home could not own it. I believe this took place because I laid hands on the painting and asked for God's blessings on it. We need to remember anything we give to the Lord, He will use when we honor Him. Like Moses in Exodus 4:2 when God simply asked, "What is in your hand?"

James 5:16 NKJV
"The effective, fervent prayer of a righteous man avails much."

Spirit-filled believers are righteous because of His righteousness, and because we are, we can boldly come into the throne room of God with our prayers and offerings. If the Lord can use the dust and dirt of this earth to make one of His finest and most treasured possessions (man and woman) then He can use anything we give Him. God is a giver, but He also likes to receive gifts, too.

I AM THE WAY
John 14:6

4
Using
THE GIFT

I heard about an artist touring group called (of all things), the "Artist Touring Association" (ATA). This was a group of professional artists who traveled the country selling their work in malls. It was a popular thing back then, and they had a show in different parts of the country every week. It was a great way to gain exposure for my work and see the country at the same time. By the end of the first year, I had refined my skill immensely as an artist and the money wasn't bad either.

While doing a show in Pompano Beach, Florida, a crowd gathered around me in the middle of the mall as I painted a brilliant sunset on canvas. As I stepped back to get a full view of the piece and critique any necessary adjustments, I could hear all the "Oohs" and "Ahhhs" from the people around me, which not only filled my ears but also my heart.

I had to get some supplies out of the van in the parking lot of the mall, so I put my brushes down and walked outside the mall. I began patting myself on the back telling myself, "Yeah Hahlbohm! You're alright! You do some mighty fine paintings!"

As I opened the mall doors and went outside, I saw a magnificent sunset in the skies above me. It was breathtaking, as are many of Florida's sunsets, but this one seemed to be especially magnificent. I continued walking toward the van, analyzing the sunset before me, storing all the colors, the contrasts and details inside my head for future reference to paint at some point. Once I gathered all the "art info," I then looked at the sunset from a regular point of view. It was beautiful, maybe the best sunset I would ever see.

I remember thinking to myself, My God, what a beautiful sunset. Instantly, I heard an almost thunderous voice of God shout, "Yes it is . . . and don't you ever forget that the best you can do is only a poor imitation of what I do every day!"

Besides the fact that immediately my head shrunk back to its original size, this was the first time I ever heard God's voice in a stern, powerful manner. It was almost like a correcting father would scold his child. I felt so ashamed of myself for being so puffed up by listening to the praise of people. How could I have boasted so brashly (even to myself) over a talent and gift given to me? I never went to school to learn how to paint. I never took classes of any kind. I simply always had the talent. It was in the purest sense of the word gift. How could anyone be boastful over something given to them?

I have never forgotten that moment nor what the Lord said, not even to this day some forty years later. God always has

> ### LION AND LAMB
> Isaiah 11:6

been the true artist within me. I create because it comes from the Creator. All the inspiration I use to create a painting comes from Him, through the Holy Spirit, and onto my hands. God created it all first. Yes, indeed, the very best I could ever do would only be a poor imitation of what He has done for thousands of years. This lesson was fully noted and inscribed deeply within my spirit.

To further prove this point (of who is the real artist inside), I believe the Lord led me to paint seascapes as well. I have always loved the water. That's why I moved to Florida; however, I wasn't always able to paint what I loved so much. For that to happen, I had to learn another lesson from the Lord.

I remember the first time I tried painting water. It was a disaster! I had such a passion for the sea and longed to paint it on canvas, but I didn't have the ability in that area at all. I mean . . . none. Over and over I would try, to no avail, and finally gave up and went back to painting landscapes, barns, florals, and the like.

A few months went by and one day as I placed another blank canvas upon the easel to paint, I felt the overwhelming urge to paint the sea again. Knowing I had absolutely no ability in that area, I dismissed the urge at first, but I still felt a strong desire to paint it this time. It seemed as though the Holy Spirit was edging me on, pushing me from behind saying, "Come on, come on. We can do this. Let's go."

I finally gave in and the seascape just flowed from my brush (pun intended).

USING THE GIFT

It literally just flowed with no effort at all. How could it happen that I could go from absolutely zero ability, to remarkable knowledge and ability with no practice or training? How? God! That is the only possible answer. It is simply and purely a gift from God.

Romans 4:17
"Even God, who quickeneth the dead and calleth those things which are not, as though they were."

My ability to paint water prior to God's touch definitely fell into the "Not" category. As hard as I tried, as earnest as my desire and love of the sea were, the ability proved not to be there at all. Yet, with the touch of the Master's hand, those things which were impossible are now possible.

Of all the paintings I have ever done, I have created and sold more seascapes by far than any other. I have painted in front of hundreds of thousands of people in the malls during my fifteen-year tour. If you talked to anyone of them who remembered me painting, they would tell you the water scenes just flowed off my brush. I say this not in a boastful spirit (I learned my lesson very well from the sunsets) but from a humble spirit, because I know the talent comes from the Lord, and of Him I shall boast all the days of my life!

Now when I boast, I do not say, "Yeah, Hahlbohm, you're pretty good." Instead, I boldly claim, "Yes, Lord, Thou art the Creator of ALL things. Your ability is beyond compare to enable me to use my feeble hands and create such beautiful works of art. Thou art the Master Artist!"

The astounding thing is that while creating all those "out at sea" seascapes, I had never been out at sea even once. Yet, I would paint the most intense raging storms from the depths of the oceans with full knowledge of something I had neither seen nor experienced. I had many sailors who were seasoned maritime men and who lived out at sea remark at the accuracy I painted of the seas. Tugboat captains, Naval officers, and seamen alike all exclaimed that the paintings were, in the smallest detail, exactly as it was out there. Many called me a liar when I told them I had never been out at sea.

So how did I acquire that knowledge and acute accuracy? The answer is, I never did, but I knew the One who not only walked on waters like these, but who also created them. With the help and guidance of the Holy Spirit, there is nothing we cannot do together in faith, even those things we know nothing of.

The Lord told me (in that still quiet voice inside) from the very first painting I had done for Him, that if I let pride enter in, He could not use me. I had forgotten that when I did the sunsets, but I was quickly corrected. However, from that time forward, I kept those words and His chastisement close to my heart that I should not fail or need to be reminded again.

One of the most prestigious outdoor shows in the country at the time was the Coconut Grove Show near Miami, Florida, which I attended in 1978. It was here I hooked up with one of the largest publishing companies at that time, Scafa-Tornabene Art Publishing Company.

They seemed to be very interested in my work, particularly the religious ones, even though both Clair and her husband,

> **NOTHING IS IMPOSSIBLE**
> Luke 1:37

One night I dreamed
I was walking along the beach with the Lord.
Many scenes from my life flashed across the sky.
In each scene I noticed footprints in the sand.
Sometimes there were two sets of footprints,
other times there were one set of footprints.

This bothered me because I noticed
that during the low periods of my life,
when I was suffering from
anguish, sorrow or defeat,
I could see only one set of footprints.

So I said to the Lord,
'You promised me Lord,
that if I followed you,
you would walk with me always.
But I have noticed that during the most
trying periods of my life there have only been
one set of footprints in the sand.
Why, when I needed you most,
you have not been there for me?'

The Lord replied,
'The times when you have seen
only one set of footprints in the sand,
is when I carried you.'

Dino, were Jewish. Although they loved my work, the paintings I was doing at the time were all in blue. They had concerns, since the trend at that time was in earth tones of orange, brown, and yellow. Nonetheless, Clair went with her instincts (pushed by God, no doubt) and took ten of them, which was quite unusual, since I was an unknown artist. Her hunches proved to be right, and within that year, they were selling my work around the world in thirty-three other countries besides the United States. I was among the top Christian artists in the country.

I continued doing the mall art shows across the country. Each week, I was setting up my display and gathering large crowds around me as I painted. At one particular show, out of the corner of my eye, I saw a lady gently leave a note at my easel. Usually the notes read, "God bless you in your work," or perhaps just a simple "Thank you." Most of the people did not want to disturb the artist, so they left me a simple note of their appreciation for me to read at my earliest convenience.

As I completed one last brushstroke, I turned to thank the woman who just left the note. She was not there. There was no sign of her, which was odd, because I could see for hundreds of feet around me. It was as if she simply disappeared. Puzzled and confused, I decided to grab a cup of coffee and read the note she left on the easel. I sat down and opened the note and there it was: "Footprints in the Sand."

The poem brought tears to my eyes and made my spirit leap. Such beautiful inspiration and I had no one to thank. The

FOOTPRINTS IN THE SAND
© 1979 Scafa Tornebene

more I tried to recall the event, the more I realized I never saw the woman's face. In my mind, the glimpse I saw appeared to be an older woman. Yet, it did happen. I had the note in my hands. Was it an angel unaware, as my mother often called them? I do not know. All I know is that God placed it before me and wanted me to have it published and share it with the world. That was exactly what I did. I called my publisher to try and find who the author was, and she replied that it was never copyrighted in any legal office. By the end of 1978, I had created a painting for that poem, and the rest is history (as they say).

Some time later, I found out that the poem was written in 1938 by Mary Stevenson. I had a chance to talk to Mary many years after it was published and asked her if she was the one who left the note on my easel. She told me she was not. It's probably just as well, because my next question would have been, "How did you disappear like that?"

Mary Stevenson passed away within a year after I talked to her. I always thought it was so sad that she never got the full recognition she deserved. Then perhaps, she never wanted the recognition. She was not distraught over losing recognition, she was very happy it finally got published and blessed people around the world. I believe it was that kind of genuine humility and love that promoted the Lord to make it so. I am sure when she entered heaven, the Lord gave Mary the rewards she richly deserved but never received down here.

Early on in my own personal art ministry, I remember the Lord told me the visions and inspirations given to me were never meant for me alone, but they were to be shared, passed on to the rest of the body of Christ as well. The blessing from the Holy Spirit passes through the artwork the Lord has given me to those whom the Lord speaks. I have heard from many people who have felt the blessing from many of the paintings I created, and for that I give all the honor and glory to the Master Artist and Creator, Jesus Christ.

It is all about the giving, because by giving, we receive. Jesus was our perfect example for this. All that we have and shall have is because Christ gave His life in our behalf.

Luke 17:33

"Whosoever shall seek to save his life shall lose it; and whosoever shall lose his life shall preserve it."

You (the body of Christ) are the intended receivers of any gift. For example, if I do not put those visions given to me on canvas and give them to the world, those visions die within me, and so do the blessings. However, by freely giving the gift to others, God brings life to that vision as He intended from the start. The more it is shared, the more it continues to grow and be a blessing just as it had thousands of years ago with the feeding of five thousand.

Matthew 15:36-38 NIV

"Then he took the seven loaves and the fish, and when he had given thanks, he broke them and gave them to the disciples, and they in turn to the people. They all ate and were satisfied. Afterward the disciples picked up seven basketfuls of broken pieces that were left over. The number of those who ate was four thousand men, besides women and children."

The ones who may receive the visions and or blessings from God are merely messengers . . . like postmen. The letter (blessing) is not meant for them, but it is to be delivered to the ones intended, you! As for me, I am glad the Lord lets me peek inside those letters before passing them on.

THY WILL BE DONE
Luke 22:41-43

USING THE GIFT

5
Through
THE STORM

By this time, we made our way across the country and into California. Upon arrival, I found I could not produce the paintings fast enough. I was selling my artwork in the art shows before the paintings were completed, and I was pretty fast by now. We thought to ourselves, Thar is Gold in them thar hills, by golly! and for the first couple years, it seemed so.

We found a place to live in Anaheim, California, which was only two blocks from Disney Land. The kids were quite happy about that, and we took the three of them with us whenever possible in between art shows. The Lord was blessing us abundantly until I took my eyes off of Him and began relying on my own provision instead of the source that provided it.

My God Room visits became fewer and fewer because I didn't have the time; I was trying to keep up with the art demand. God had taken second place in my life, and He was not happy with that seating.

Soon the money and sales began to dwindle lower and lower with each art show we attended. Instead of taking more time for the Lord, I just tried to increase my workflow, working longer hours to create the paintings. Financially, I finally got to a point of desperation. We were two months behind on our rent (in California that is a

lot of dollars), and the lady who was renting the house we owned in New York suddenly stopped paying her rent. The van wasn't running at 100 percent, and I had to do the maintenance work that was needed to keep it on the road because I was trying to make more money.

Finally, I decided I would ask the Lord to help us out and even began praying over each painting on the display racks before the show. Surely NOW God would heard our plea and come to our rescue. No, not a word or heavenly finger to help us out. God heard alright, and He saw as well, but He wanted more a lot more. We do not put God on a leash; He puts a leash on us and for good reason. We cannot put God in a box and only take Him out when we need His hand. God is a jealous God, always has been, and He must be first in our lives. If He is not, then He may create situations and pressure until He becomes first. He does not do this out of anger but rather love. He knows the only way we can obtain His blessings is by having no other Gods before Him.

Weeks went on and we were going deeper and deeper in debt without any response or help from God until I finally turned to God one night. Looking up into the dark night sky, I said, "God, You know our situation. You see us here and hear our prayers. I know You do, but You have not lifted a finger to help. We have prayed over the situation and over the paintings to support ourselves,

AT THE HELM
Psalm 93:4

but it is as if those prayers fell on deaf ears. Don't you care?"

I waited for some kind of response, but none came. I closed the conversation by saying, "OK, God. If You don't care about us, then neither do I care about You any longer." With that, I shut God out of my thoughts and told myself, "Well, I guess I have to do it on my own." Big mistake!

My wife back then still held onto her faith. She had no answer to God's silence through all this, but she still went to church each week and took the kids with her. Each time she would go, she would ask me if I wanted to come. My response was always the same. "What for? God and I are through with one another. He doesn't care about me, nor I Him."

This went on for another few weeks, and I was getting deeper in debt. My sales dropped to nothing, and I held my ground: No more God. I did hear faintly the Lord call out to me a few times (that small inner voice again), but I snubbed it off. I didn't want to see God's face right now. I only wanted His hand, His help. If I wasn't going to receive His hand, then I didn't need to seek His face. I would move when He did!

My wife stopped asking me if I would go to church with them anymore because my answer was always the same, and she did not like to hear it. However, I began thinking to myself, This is still my family, and it is my obligation as their dad to be with them whether I believed in God anymore or not. So as they made their way out the door, I told them I would go with them. When we got to the church, there was a special speaker preaching that night named LaVerne Tripp. I never heard of him before, but I was about to, front and center!

The service started and we headed down the aisle. We sat five rows or so back

and settled in. I felt like a tiger in a cage. I squirmed in my seat as I kept looking around and not listening to the message that was being preached. I wanted no part of it. God and I were through. Then halfway through the meeting, they began taking up an offering. I told my wife I was going outside for a while and I would be back when they finished their song. When I came back in, they were in the middle of a prayer, so I stayed in the back of the church, leaned up against the wall, and waited.

The prayer ended, and there was a couple of other people in the back waiting to be seated as well. As we all began to make our way down the aisle, all of a sudden, BAM, I got shoved right back against the wall of the church. At first I thought I lost my footing because I hit pretty hard. I tried again, and, bam! I was slammed against the wall again.

Now I was perplexed. I tried one more time, and the same thing happened. This time, however, I realized it was not bad footing but something else going on. As I got slammed back against the wall the third time, I felt two large hands push me back. I could feel it so acutely that I also noticed it was not one right hand and one left hand. It was like someone in front of me was pushing me back with two distinct hands from two people. Angels?

I never saw them, yet their presence was quite well known to me. God did not want me sitting back down ignoring the message by twiddling my thumbs and looking around. He wanted my full, undivided attention, and He was going to have it one way or the other.

As LaVerne Tripp began his sermon, he stopped and looked into the congregation and saw me standing alone pinned against the wall. "I don't know why," he declared, "but the Holy Spirit is leading me to share a different message with you tonight than I had planned to talk about. I asked the Lord to send His angels to lock the doors and not let anyone leave until the Lord has said all He has come to say."

I know if those angels had not pinned me solidly against that wall, my knees would have buckled at that point, and I would have fallen to the floor. However, I was pinned, pinned tightly against the back wall all by myself. Even the ushers found their seats and were seated. I was a captive audience, fully exposed, and God wanted it that way.

When the service was over, LaVerne began to give an altar call, but before he got three words into the invitation, a woman stood up and spoke in tongues. Right after she spoke, another woman interpreted that message, and it sent chills down my spine.

"I have called you once. I have called you twice. I have called you three times and thou hast let all the things of this world separate you from Me. Thou art lukewarm and thou knowest it not. I have called thee. I have spoken to thee, and yet thou hast rejected Me. Therefore, I say unto thee, reject Me no more. Knowest not that I come quickly. Thou art not satisfied with anything! Thou art not satisfied with church! Thou art not satisfied with thy family! Thou art not satisfied with thy job! Thou art not satisfied with anything because thy problem is spiritual. Thou hast turned away from me. There was a time when thou wast close to Me. There was a time when you did speak to Me. There was a time when nothing could separate thee from Me, but thou hast become lukewarm. Therefore, I say unto thee, shake thyself and awaken! Awaken child, before it is too late and come unto Me this night lest another wear you down, thus sayeth the Lord."

The angels loosened their grip and I fled as quickly as I could down the aisle with tears streaming down my face, begging forgiveness, and feeling the Lord's arms wrap around me once again. I rededicated my life to the Lord and never forgot the mercy and forgiveness of God that dark, but glorious night.

We finally got out of California, but the Lord's prophecy was correct. A storm did fall upon me and my family. We hit the lowest point I believe we ever reached. We were homeless and picking up cans on the side of the road to feed the family. On the way from Anaheim, California, to West Virginia, we blew out twenty-two tires on the road. Even those people who were broke themselves helped us find old used tires so we could get to the show in West Virginia.

Yes, Satan was out in full force, but he was too late. I rededicated my life to Christ and I was in God's hand once again. I learned my lesson very well and I was going to make it through the storm to the other side this time. Praise the Lord for His grace and faithfulness. Where would any of us be without His divine grace?

I resumed my alone time with God as before. Most of the time, my time in the God Room was while my family was asleep or I was heading down the road to the next city. I spent hours talking to the Lord and hearing Him talk to me about everything. We tend to think the Lord only cares about the big stuff. No, He cares about the little everyday stuff too. I remember even having conversations with Him about how good that last breakfast in Ohio was, or some song I thought was just great. Yes, Christ is our Lord, the King of kings, my Savior and Master, but He is also closer than a brother. The Bible says He even calls us His friends.

John 15:15

"Henceforth I call you not servants; for the servant knoweth not what his lord doeth: but I have called you friends; for all things that I have heard of my Father I have made known unto you."

So why wouldn't I have simple and silly conversation with my best friend? God says if we draw close to Him, He will draw close to us, not just in times of peril or hardship. We can share the good times with the Lord too, even silly times every now and then. I have a close relationship with my pastor; we are each other's best friend, yet he is also my shepherd. He is appointed by God for that position, and I also reverence that in his life as well. You can be both to God, servant and friend. As a matter of fact, later on I was to do a painting based on that premise. It has been widely accepted, so I know others feel the same way.

One day as I was in my God Room traveling down the long highway heading into Saginaw, Michigan, I talked to the Lord, thanking Him once again for giving me a job to not only proclaim His name, but also to provide for my family. (The financial drought I went through had been over by

THE QUESTION
Matthew 27:22

this time.) I felt the Lord smile and said, "That's good, Danny, but it is time to get serious about your calling. My people need meat."

That took me back some. By this point in time, "Footprints in the Sand" had sold over eight million copies, and most of my work (30 or 40 pieces) was selling worldwide. I was perhaps the most well-known artist in the Bible bookstores, and Jesus was telling me now is the time to put my nose to the grindstone?

Continuing our talk together down the road, I began to see where the Lord wanted me to go. It wasn't the quantity, but the quality that needed a change. He brought before me a vision of what to paint and gave me the title for it: "The Question." He then gave me the scripture for this new painting.

Matthew 27:22

"What shall I do then with Jesus which is called Christ?"

I set up the display in the Saginaw mall, put a fresh blank canvas up on the easel, stood back, and contemplated what to paint regarding the verse Jesus had given me. Within minutes, it came to me almost as

THROUGH THE STORM

it had when I did the first painting in my basement many years ago of "The Second Coming." I began laying down the paint, stroke by stoke, and within a few hours, the painting was finished.

There was no doubt about it. This was "meat," the heart of the matter for non-believers. A question we all have to answer at one time or another is: What shall we do with Jesus which is called the Christ? Are we going to accept Him, accept that He is what He claims He is? Or are we going to reject that statement and deny Him? One way or the other, it is the question. Our answer either brings life or death to us. No other question has this magnitude. Trying to ignore it, as Pilate did by washing his hands, will not do. There is no middle ground.

Matthew 12:30 NIV
"Whoever is not with me is against me, and whoever does not gather with me scatters."

The sales on the reproductions of this painting may not have been the best, but the painting got people's attention and became the talk of the town for a while. Everyone had an opinion on this piece. Good or bad, they had a comment. It was indeed the "meat" the Lord had spoken of. There was something much deeper than just saying, "God loves you. Go in peace." Yes, God does love you indeed, and you need to remember that always, but you and I also have a responsibility with the precious gift of life God has given to us. With that life comes the "Question."

We finished the show and headed to our next show in Cincinnati, Ohio. After setting up the display in the middle of the mall, I began to create another painting of meaty substance called, "My Son . . . My Son." As I stood there painting, I opened up a silent conversation with the Lord. I said, "Lord, I enjoy working for You and doing Your will in my life, but in all honesty, I could be painting these paintings in the privacy of my home just as well as out here. Each week I have to set up and tear down, not to mention the cost and expense of traveling. I could really do a better job and produce more for You if I did not have to paint in the malls all the time."

The Lord said, "Danny, look around. Tell me what you see."

I stopped for a second, looked around and replied, "Well, I am in a mall, Lord. There are stores and a crowd of people watching me paint."

The Lord answered, "Yes, that's right. You are in the middle of a public mall, spreading My Word. What would happen if you stopped what you were doing right now, stood on a soapbox, and began preaching to all these people?"

"Well, I would probably be immediately escorted out of the mall by the security guards. The malls frown on that sort of thing being done publicly."

"Yes!" the Lord continued, "Exactly. By using the talent I have given you and doing these shows, you are not only proclaiming My name in the middle of a major public gathering, but also the people in charge actually invite you to come."

The Lord was right. I was in a prime location in most of the major malls across the country. Many of them estimated that over a hundred thousand people would come through those malls in the course of one weekend alone. I have to say, I was somewhat disappointed at not being able to paint quietly at home, but I got the point.

I can sympathize and relate to others who have God's calling, like ministers and preachers across the country. There are

indeed sacrifices that are required when following God's call. However, I know the rewards are there in the end, and even in-between. We can never out-give God. I turned back and continued painting.

About midway through the piece, I noticed a woman standing some distance away at one of the intersecting aisles in the mall. There was nothing particularly unusual about her appearance, yet she seemed to catch my eye. She leaned against the wall, as if in deep thought, as she gazed at the painting in progress from a distance. I did not think too much of it and continued to work on the piece. After a couple of days when I had finished the painting, the woman came up and introduced herself.

"Hi, my name is Ellen. You don't know me, but I am a fellow exhibitor at the show. My booth is right around the corner. I have been watching you paint this masterpiece for quite a while now, and there is something I have to tell you.

"You see a few days ago," she continued, "my life was so depressing I decided to end it all and take my life. As I was on my way out, I saw you painting this piece and for some reason, I had to stop and watch. It spoke directly to me, and I knew after seeing this painting I couldn't go through with the suicide. I felt the depth of Mary's agony through your painting, and I couldn't put my loved ones through that same agony if I were to take my life. I realized then that I loved them too, and I did have something to live for. I feel very embarrassed telling you this, and it has taken me a couple of days to gather the courage, but I needed to tell you how much your painting has touched me

MY SON... MY SON
Matthew 20:18

and turned my situation around. Actually, you saved my life."

I was speechless. I had no idea. We grabbed a cup of coffee at one of the stands in the mall and sat down to chat. I told her of the greatness of God's love and all He had done for me personally. We talked for many hours and became good friends for years afterward.

How precious is the love of God that He would inspire me to do a particular painting, have me drive miles across the land, set up in a mall to create this painting so one lonely and disheartened soul would not take her life! How could anyone ever say God does not care about us? He moves and redirects the universe in the course of normal events just to prove His love is real because He does care.

Also, I felt completely embarrassed in complaining to the Lord just days before about having to do mall shows for a living. I know the Lord understood and had compassion on me, but I still felt like crawling under the mall carpet.

The show turned out to be successful in more ways than one. Unknown to me, there was another person who had taken interest in my work, a fellow I was soon to meet at my next show.

Just a few hours away was my next exhibit in Indianapolis. The first day of the show, a young man came to me and introduced himself. He was in his early twenties and told me he had seen my work the previous week in Cincinnati. He found out that I was going to be in Indianapolis and came to see me.

He was a PK (a preacher's kid) who had grown up in the church. He knew all about Christ from a young age, how He died for our sins, and that Jesus was the only way to salvation. The young man had never truly accepted Christ into his heart, even though he pretended to because of his father. By being around other Christians, he had developed a rather acute ability to block out any words of conviction in regards to accepting Jesus into his life. That is, until he stumbled into the mall and saw my work there.

He told me, "If you had shown these paintings in our church, I would not have noticed them. My "automated defense mechanism" would have shot up immediately as I entered the church, and my role playing would have begun. Instead, there were your paintings in the middle of the mall, of all places, and my defenses were down! I was unguarded, never expecting to find God's Word being spread through art in such a public place."

The young man continued, "I had my defenses down to a science, but instead of hearing the Word of God, now I was seeing the Word. I had no defense for that. All the things I had been taught suddenly seemed clear. These visions were now there visually, along with the sermons I had heard. Before I realized it, I was crying and accepting the Lord as my Savior."

He wiped the tears from his eyes and continued, "I just had to drive up here to thank you for tearing down the blockade Satan had so cleverly placed inside me. Thank you for those sermons on canvas."

That was another exclamation point in answer to my question, of why I had to be in malls with my art. So often we question God about His ways. The truth is that we do not see the big picture God has in store for us.

I have been given numerous visions from God to paint; however, there was one time in my life when a large array of visions came to me in a very unusual way. As I was driving down the road to pick up some supplies in Columbus, Ohio, I was peering up into the sky, checking out the cloud formations, trying to remember and reconstruct them in my head for a future painting.

As I looked up at the clouds, suddenly I began viewing some awesome artwork, artwork that I had never seen before. They were beautiful and I could not help but admire the content and detail within these pieces. I do not remember the exact number, but as far as I can recall, it was eight to twelve pieces. As I looked more carefully, I realized something amazing. Although I had never seen these pieces before, there was a style about them that seemed familiar, but I could not quite put my finger on it. Then it hit me like a ton of hard, cold bricks. It was my style! These were paintings I had not created yet and didn't have the expertise to do. I was looking into the future at paintings yet to be created!

When the "slide show" subsided and faded, I tried to recall those works again in my head. I could not remember one of them in detail, only that they were simply wonderful and far beyond my skills at the time. I began asking God what this was all about and why I could not remember any of the paintings clearly. There was no answer. It puzzled me for quite some time. How I longed to remember those pieces in detail to create them on canvas. Why had God shown them to me and then erased them from my mind?

A few years later, I met an author who had a near-death experience. She claimed that while she was legally pronounced dead, she was taken to heaven and shown some wondrous things. Among them, she was shown her mission in life and told she needed to return back to her body and fulfill what the Lord had called her to do.

In speaking with her, she brought up one interesting point that may have some bearing on the answer to my slide show of visions in the car. She said that after she was shown her mission and why she needed to return, the Lord immediately erased it from her mind. Bewildered, she asked why and was given this answer: If she was permitted to remember her exact mission, she would think of nothing else, and end up missing out on the many smaller events she also needed to learn and experience on her walk down here.

I wondered if that answer also applied in my case. Had God shown me those paintings to get me fired up, as it were, and then the details removed so I, too, would not be sidetracked? The creation of those paintings would therefore need to take its natural course in due time, rather than immediately as my instincts would have insisted. I tend to have tunnel vision in goals before me.

I never really did receive an answer to that question. I simply had to have faith that in God's timing, He would reveal the answer. There have been a couple of paintings since that time that have come to fruition regarding that vision. I know now in having created those pieces, I did not have the expertise needed back then to create them. God's perfect timing was needed, and apparently so was the vision beforehand.

After being on the road constantly for fifteen years doing mall art shows, the Lord finally granted my wish and I began painting at home. However, all that constant traveling took its toll on my family, and soon I was divorced. I moved to Florida. Many years later, I married a wonderful Christian woman (Diana) who has been my life support, both physically and spiritually.

One evening in my home I was praying about a need in my life and bringing it before the Lord. I don't remember now what it was specifically, but I remember it was a great need and I was going on and on about it.

I was on my knees with my head bent down and hands clasped when I felt as though the Lord put His hand under my chin. Picking it up to meet His eyes, He said, "All these things I have desired to do for you, but remember, my child, seek My face, not just My hand."

I was so moved by that moment that I decided I had to paint it. My wife, a professional photographer, was visiting her family in Kansas. She had a number of models she had used. I asked her to take some shots of Becca in the poses I needed in order to paint the piece.

SEEK MY FACE
Psalm 27:8

THROUGH THE STORM

HOLY SPIRIT

The Lord gave me a vision of the Holy Spirit descending. As He did, I could see His robe of white and gold flutter behind him, almost like white wings. I can see why those who saw it themselves in the Bible said it was like a dove descending.

Matthew 3:16
"And Jesus, when he was baptized, went up straightway out of the water: and, lo, the heavens were opened unto him, and he saw the Spirit of God descending like a dove, and lighting upon him."

NO GREATER LOVE

I live in Florida. One day, I was at the beach reflecting on the great love God showed in sending His only Son for me. The Lord then opened the skies and this is the vision I saw.

John 15:13
"Greater love hath no man than this, that a man lay down his life for his friends."

GIFT FROM ABOVE

Roses generally signify "love." Yet if you look closer you will see the real meaning of love: the Holy Spirit (in the water drops) and the blood drops of Christ's sacrifice. This kind of love can only come from above, for God is love.

James 1:17
"Every good gift and every perfect gift is from above, and cometh down from the Father of lights, with whom is no variableness, neither shadow of turning."

HOMAGE

What a glorious day, for unto us a child is given: God's child, His only Son, to take away the sins of the world forever! Yes, every knee shall bow and give the Lord His due homage and reverence.

Philippians 2:10
"That at the name of Jesus every knee should bow, of things in heaven, and things in earth, and things under the earth."

BODY OF CHRIST

I wanted to show how we all make up the body of Christ. Unfortunately, I could not include every profession within the piece but tried to pick out a range that suited the painting. However, every true believer is within the body of Christ, and every gift and calling is important to Him.

Romans 12:5
"So we, being many, are one body in Christ, and every one members one of another."

YOUR MOVE

God is, without doubt, the master chessman. Although God does not consider life a 'game,' He does move His celestial chess pieces around for His will to be done. God has made His move, He gave us His Son in place of our sin. Now it is our move. What will you do? Will you accept His gift or reject it?

Matthew 27:22 NIV
"What shall I do, then, with Jesus who is called the Messiah?"

WISE AND FOOLISH BUILDERS

Matthew 7:24-27

"Therefore whosoever heareth these sayings of mine, and doeth them, I will liken him unto a wise man, which built his house upon a rock: And the rain descended, and the floods came, and the winds blew, and beat upon that house; and it fell not: for it was founded upon a rock. And every one that heareth these sayings of mine, and doeth them not, shall be likened unto a foolish man, which built his house upon the sand: And the rain descended, and the floods came, and the winds blew, and beat upon that house; and it fell: and great was the fall of it."

UNTO US

I used two of our church members for this painting. However, unknown to all of us, and to them as well, Chris's wife Melinda was pregnant at the time and they had their own child nine months later.

Isaiah 9:6
"For unto us a child is born, unto us a son is given."

A Higher CALLING

6

I owned a house in Sarasota and a 29-foot sailboat that Di and I used to go out on almost every weekend. However, after a number of years, once again, my income began to decline rapidly. I had to leave my home, sell my sailboat, and move to the small town of North Port, Florida, where we began renting. We stayed afloat (pardon the pun) a couple of years, but the decline in finances continued. Soon it was apparent we were about to become homeless. I prayed about it often but still the finances kept declining in a downward spin.

I found myself at a spiritual crossroads much like I had in California. We prayed about it, but it seemed the more we prayed, the less income we received. As I prayed harder, the finances dropped even lower. Finally, I fell on my knees one day and looked up toward the heavens and asked why? Why did it seem God was working against my prayers? I knew very well He heard my pleas, but instead of helping me rise above them, we kept sinking deeper and deeper in debt.

I remembered my favorite verse in Job and declared it audibly:

Job 13:15 NKJV
"Though He slay me, yet will I trust in Him."

SELF PORTRAIT
1 Corinthians 6:19

More importantly, I meant it now with every fiber of my being. I told my wife of my declaration to God and she agreed with me. Our simple stance of faith was all that was needed to unleash God and behold the mighty power of His hand!

So now you are probably thinking I am going to say something like: "All of a sudden the doors swung open and money started pouring in!" Actually, quite the opposite happened.

Instead, the bottom fell out completely, and we were forced to leave the house we were renting because we could no longer make the payments. Still, we knew we had to hold fast to our declaration and promise to the Lord. Perhaps we experienced the same mindset Peter had when Jesus asked Him if he was going to leave Him too.

John 6:68
"Then Simon Peter answered him, Lord, to whom shall we go? thou hast the words of eternal life."

Indeed, without Christ, and without our faith . . . where would we go? To whom would we turn?

I felt almost like I was reliving California all over again, and perhaps in some circumstances, I was. The difference, the deciding difference, was that instead of turning my back on God because I did not see His hand helping me, this time I clung hard to faith. Perhaps in a way, God was giving me another opportunity with the same circumstances, an opportunity to pass the "faith test" instead of failing miserably as I had in California.

The enemy kept whispering in my ear, "You have been praying now for months on end, and where has it gotten you? The more you pray, the further in debt you become. You see that! That is the facts, Jack. Not this weak promise of hope you desperately cling to."

The more those evil spirits whispered, the more I clung onto Job 13:15. Like a song jingle you just can't get rid of, I played it over and over in my soul. No, this time I am going to follow God even until the end, and if He does indeed slay me, still I will trust Him!"

The very next day, my wife went to her usual woman's meeting in our local church. During the meeting, the pastor's wife told the women to pair up for prayer and teaching. My wife's partner was Patrice, someone she did not know. After the meeting, she and Patrice were talking, and one thing led to another when Diana mentioned we were going through some hard times.

Patrice asked if I was a military veteran. Diana said I was, and Patrice began telling Diana about some benefits we had not known about that could help us in our situation.

Patrice then told Diana that God directed her to leave her state of New Hampshire to come to Florida for a while. She said the Lord gave her the names of three military veterans she was to contact before she came back. One of those names was Danny.

Through the contacts Patrice gave us, we met another woman in the veteran's program who was specifically looking to relocate military veterans who were losing their housing within that month. She set up an appointment for us to see the head of the housing program, who met with us and four other couples. By the end of the day, we had a housing voucher issued by the government. All of this took place in a matter of a few days, a process which usually took six to eight months. This expedited shuffle was extremely needed. As you are about to find out, God's timing is so perfect that it's truly amazing!

In March of 2011 we moved into the government housing the Lord provided. I didn't realize at the time this housing was only three blocks from the hospital into which I would soon be admitted, and that one of the leading doctors for the illness I had was on staff at that hospital. I was unaware that my life was in grave danger. Physically, I felt fine. I had small aches and pains that normally come with being sixty-one years of age, but I didn't have anything that would appear life threatening. I didn't know these things, but God indeed did, and He was arranging the "chess pieces" for a victorious final outcome.

For a couple of weeks, I began to feel small, sharp pains in my stomach. I didn't think much of the pain at the time, assuming it was merely a stomach virus. I took some medicine for it and decided to wait and see if it would pass, as viruses usually do. It never did. The pain got increasingly worse, and I began having bad bouts of vomiting and inflammations. Realizing this was no virus, my wife rushed me three blocks away to the emergency room at the hospital.

After some quick observations and tests, they told us they had to operate immediately.

ARMOR OF GOD
Ephesians 6:14-17

Stand therefore, having girded your waist with truth, having put on the breastplate of righteousness, and having shod your feet with the preparation of the gospel of peace; above all, taking the shield of faith with which you will be able to quench all the fiery darts of the wicked one. And take the helmet of salvation, and the sword of the Spirit, which is the word of God;

Ephesians 6:14-17

Armor of God

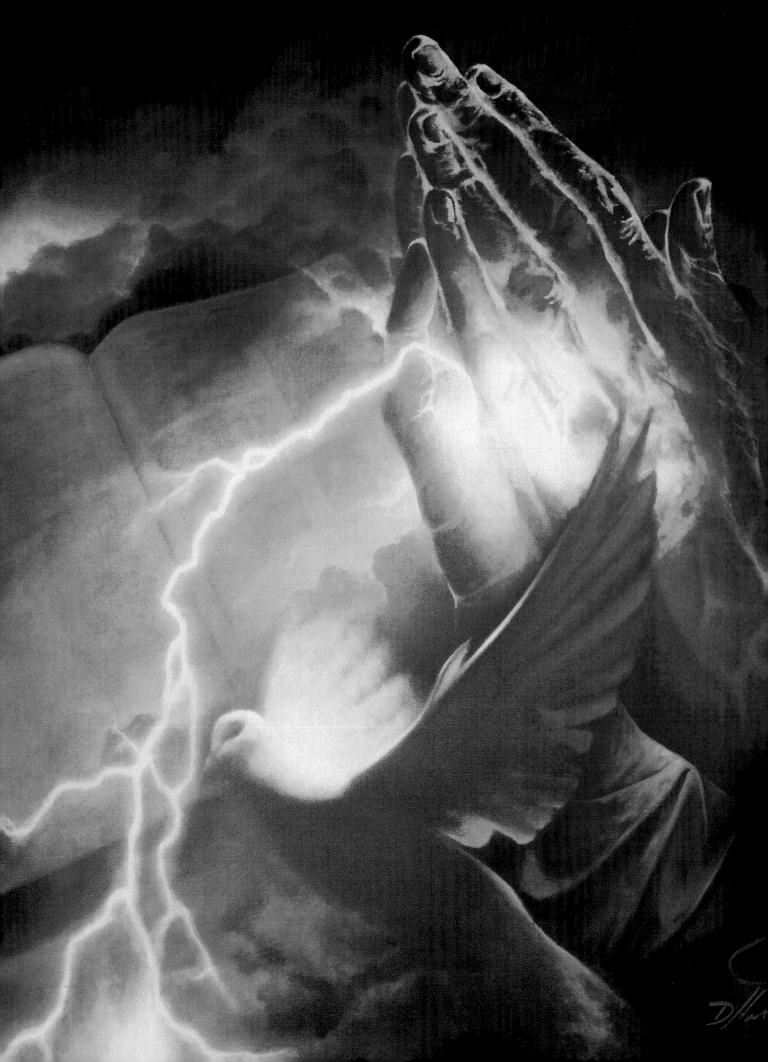

What I had was diverticulitis. They said my chances of surviving, in the condition I was in, were only thirteen percent. My chances would have been much better if I had been admitted within hours of the intestinal wall bursting, but I waited almost a week, thinking it was just a stomach flu. The doctors could not believe I was still alive, much less conscious, because the infection had spread throughout my entire stomach area.

I thank God for the doctor we had. He seemed more like an angel than a surgeon. He displayed so much confidence, I knew he was sent by God to help me in my dilemma. However, my wife needed something more. As they wheeled me down the hall, we passed by the hospital chapel and hanging on the wall was one of my works of art, "Power of Prayer." What are the odds that one of my prints would make it into this small hospital chapel in Punta Gorda, Florida? We knew at that moment that God had us exactly where we were supposed to be. God's signature was all over this place as He seemed to declare, "I've got you in the palm of My hand; it's going to be all right."

It took several hours in the operating room to clean it all up, and they had to remove part of my intestines as well. When the operation was finished, they wheeled me to a separate intensive care room. I am not sure how long I was out, but when I came to, I had a very unusual spiritual experience that lasted only a minute before I drifted back into unconsciousness. This experience would change my life from that point on.

When I gained consciousness, I was looking up at the wall in the ICU

> ### POWER OF PRAYER
> #### Mark 11:24

room. On the wall was a TV playing a program. All of a sudden the picture on the screen came to a stop, like time was standing still. Although there was no one in the room or within eyesight, I became aware of a discussion taking place regarding my life. This was by far no ordinary conversation. It was not the doctors nor the staff talking. In fact, the voices were not human at all. The conversation was all around me, but no one was there. It was purely a spiritual exchange, I could sense that within my own spirit.

It was a conversation I did not and could not hear. It was a conversation in which I could not see the participants. It was, however, a conversation where my existence on this earth was being determined and discussed by spiritual beings.

One might say, "It was probably just the drugs." Yes, I had been given morphine, but morphine did not cause this experience. I can say this because afterward, for almost three weeks, I was on morphine and knew exactly what the drug and side-effects felt like. So with complete assurance, I can tell you that this "conversation vision" was not due to the morphine. I was confused, but not because of the drugs.

As I experienced this supernatural event taking place before my eyes, I cried out and asked God, "What is this, Lord? What do You need me to do in my life? I don't understand."

The conversation never stopped nor was it interrupted by my questions. It continued like I was not even there. It was almost like a three-year-old child tugging at a parent's pant leg asking, "What's wrong, Daddy?" only to be ignored by the parent due to the serious nature of the discussion. Finally, after a few more seconds, I drifted back into unconsciousness again.

When I awoke hours later, I began to

pray, "Lord, what was that all about? Was it a conversation? Who was speaking? What did they say, Lord?" Once again, God seemed to ignore my questions regarding any details of that conversation except to tell me my life was not my own. I was given an extension on my life, and from this point forward, I was to live my life for others, not for myself or my career.

For almost six decades, I had tried my best to be a good and faithful servant as the Bible says, but God wanted more. The demands and stakes were higher now. He wanted His child. Just as He told me many years berfore, to seek His face more than His hands, He was now telling me He wanted my face more than simply my hands. God wanted to build a better, closer bond with me as His child, not just His servant.

In hindsight, I believe my near-death experience was a sort of additional baptism. Being a born-again child of God also made me a priest of God in His sight as well.

1 Peter 2:9

"But ye are a chosen generation, a royal priesthood, an holy nation, a peculiar people; that ye should shew forth the praises of him who hath called you out of darkness into his marvellous light."

Perhaps this additional baptism (the operation) in some way was preparing me for the task ahead, but to do so I needed to be closer, much closer to Him than ever before. Spending time alone with Him (worshipful "God Room" times of priestly communion), was to be as frequent and as necessary as breathing the air around me.

My servitude from that point forward has taken on an entirely new meaning, and with it, a much greater demand.. Remember, the Bible says, "To whom much is given

much shall be required" (see Luke 12:48).

With any extra blessing comes extra responsibility. Even so, God never places us where He has not prepared and paved the way ahead of us beforehand. Somewhere in that private conversation, it was agreed that I was capable for the task. Remember, too, God does not call the equipped; He equips the called. It always has been, and forever shall be, all about Christ and His ability and strength, not ours. He is the equipper needed for any task given.

I believe God allowed me to go through this in order to obtain a small glimpse in what secretly takes place on our behalf behind spiritually closed doors. Maybe it happened so that I could relate this miraculous event to you for your understanding and benefit as well.

I am sure there are those who will simply write off my experience as being drug-induced. This is no great surprise; people have been writing off God's miracles for centuries in one way or another. However, I know within my very soul what took place, even though I cannot explain it or prove its validity. I guess some might call that faith, or as the apostle Paul once explained it:

2 Timothy 1:12 NIV

"I know whom I have believed , and am convinced that he is able to guard what I have entrusted to him for that day."

Here again is another example of why it is important to spend quality alone time with the Lord and stay in close contact with Him every chance we get. The Lord, through the Holy Spirit, will give you the gift of discernment if you ask. It is through this gift that the Lord (who knows all) lets us know what is true and what is not.

Matthew 7:7

"Ask, and it shall be given you; seek, and ye shall find; knock, and it shall be opened unto you."

I have no doubt that similar supernatural interventions and secret spiritual discussions over our lives happen all the time. I believe the Lord intervenes in our behalf continuously, thwarting the devil's plans. We just never physically see these assaults taking place or are fully aware of them. In my particular encounter, I happened to wake up and get a cloudy view of one such conversation. Although I didn't understand it then, and don't fully understand it now, I know it was indeed heavenly entities who were having a discussion and who made a resolution in my behalf.

God intervenes and protects us hundreds of times during our lives, and many times we are never privileged to know about it. There are full-scale battles taking place every day over our souls which we never see, hear, or are aware of, yet they exist. Oh yes, my friend, they do exist indeed! This was just one I happened to witness through a "dark dimly lit glass," similar to what Paul said in 1 Corinthians 13:12. Although it was hazy at best, still it was a crystal clear example of how much God cares and watches over us throughout our lives.

I believe if you view the picture under the spiritual microscope, you may see through that "dimly lit glass" Paul talked about, a tad bit clearer:

1. He brought a woman from over a thousand miles away to seek me by name and through her, He revealed the connections and information that enabled us to be where God wanted us to be.

2. God answered our financial prayer of need by *decreasing* our income; thus, placing us in a housing development only open to tenants with low-income.

3. That housing location was only three blocks away from a hospital which connected me directly to the leading physician who took care of patients with my particular affliction. Any further and the doctors said I would not have made it.

4. God placed one of my own paintings in the hospital chapel as His signature, assuring us everything would work out fine because we were in His hands.

Now I can fully understand the Scripture that highlights God's foreknowledge and advance preparation for His own:

Deuteronomy 1:33

"Who went in the way before you, to search you out a place to pitch your tents in . . ."

If God doesn't care, then He did a whole lot of work and physical manipulation down here for nothing. No, I think it shows quite clearly just how much God does care and how far He is willing to go for our benefit and well-being. God does pay attention to our seemingly insignificant and mundane lives. We just need to trust and put our faith on the line, fully standing behind His Word, declaring it without hesitation.

Yes, like Job said thousands of years ago, "Though He slay me, yet will I trust Him." Dare to echo that statement, then stand back and imagine God's mighty hand writing His signature across your life in bright, bold, blood-red letters.

O yes, one more small detail to round this out. Right after the operation, our income immediately shot up, which made us ineligible for government housing, so we had to move. Once again, the Lord stretched forth His hand.

During a physical therapy session in which my wife was enrolled, she was told of a rental vacancy. In fact, it was her therapist who was moving out and (you guessed it) at the exact time our housing lease expired. This new condo was to be the "birth place" for the God Room and writing of this book.

Yes, God does care even about the smallest, most minute details of our lives. He is never too busy, and we are never too small. The Lord has declared us to be His personal "Masterpieces" and I can tell you firsthand, we (artists) hover over our masterpieces to protect them, for they are very dear to us.

Ephesians 2:10 NLT
"For we are God's masterpiece."

Jeremiah 1:5 NIV
"Before I formed you in the womb I knew you, before you were born I set you apart."

Luke 12:7 NIV
"Indeed, the very hairs of your head are all numbered. Don't be afraid; you are worth more than many sparrows."

BORN AGAIN
Jeremiah 1:5

7
GOD
Room

Coming straight out of the hospital from a major operation, I was unable to do anything for myself. I was barely able to eat real food again, and my dear, loving wife had to do everything for me. After a couple of weeks, I was able to sit up and soon my wife would wheel me onto our back lanai (small porch) that overlooked a beautiful setting on the premises.

Those daily sessions alone with God became known as my "God Room" experience. I would use that term when I wanted to be wheeled out there. To me, that was exactly what it was. There was nothing to hinder: no one around but God and me overlooking a beautiful area as we talked together, bonding.

I love my morning chats with the Lord. One morning out there with a cup of coffee in hand, I began my first God-Room lesson. Sitting on the back porch, I was captured by the the beauty of the lake, with birds flying by and small fish jumping every now and then below. I began thanking God for such a glorious day and being able to enjoy all His handiwork before me. As I began reflecting and taking it all in with the Lord, suddenly, a movie I had seen recently came to mind.

In this movie, "The Edge," starring Anthony Hopkins and Alex Baldwin, one particular scene was the climax of the film.

> ### ALL HAIL KING JESUS
> 1 Timothy 6:15

Both actors were being pursued and hunted by an 800-pound grizzly bear. All they had to fight with was a simple jackknife and some long branches. Anthony began to tell how hundreds of years earlier Indians killed bears using only a spear made of wood. Exhausted from running and almost being killed by the bear, Alex said, "I don't know. Just because they did it, doesn't mean we can. We are not trained to do that sort of thing."

Then Anthony Hopkins made this classic statement: "What one man can do, another can do."

Alex still denied that they could. Then Anthony insisted that Alex repeat those words, "What one man can do, another can do." Finally, Alex said it and Anthony tells him to say it again and again until Alex shouts out in a confident and victorious voice, "WHAT ONE MAN CAN DO, ANOTHER CAN DO!"

They confronted the bear; he charged after them, and ended up being impaled on the staffs they made. They defeated this 800-pound bear with only a couple of sharp sticks because they believed they could. This was almost a modern David and Goliath story.

As I thought about this, while sitting there sipping my coffee, I realized why God had brought that scene to my attention. This was, and is, the very basis and foundation of our walk with God. What God has done for one, He will do for me and you!

So many of us read about Moses, David, or Abraham and say, "Yeah, that was great, but I am not Moses." Well, if you read the story about Moses in the Bible, even Moses did not believe he was "a Moses" in the beginning. He had the same mentality and attitude most of us have that "I am no one special. You must have me mistaken for someone else, Lord." We simply cannot believe we are uniquely important to God, that is until we experience something similar to what I did. Then we realize how special to we are to God. Very special indeed.

Whatever God has done for me or used me for, He can also use you for, and perhaps even greater and more spectacular things. All you need to do is say, "Here I am, Lord. Use me." I promise you, He will!

As you read this book, apply it to your own life. The Bible says God is a respecter of no man. That means all are equal in God's eyes. When we leave here, God will not look upon Moses, David, or Joshua any differently, nor will He love them any more than He will love you and me. The only difference is the callings we have on our lives. Some callings may appear greater in our eyes than others, but that is not how God sees them at all.

1 Timothy 4:14 NKJV
"Do not neglect the gift that is in you."

Use your gifts, your calling that God has given you. He has a specialized gift customized just for you. God has given each of us a particular measure of faith to complete the tasks at hand.

You may say to yourself, "Yeah, but I do not have a calling. I am just a housewife, or a secretary, or a store clerk." Really? Let me ask you one simple question: Do you love someone? There is nothing (even the world acknowledges this) more powerful than love, real love. With love, we encourage others to do better, to be better, to love others in return, and to bring light into an otherwise dark existence.

Did you know that when you help, love or encourage others and they go on to bless others, whatever reward they reap is assigned to your account as well in the Kingdom of God? I imagine Billy Graham's mother never expected her son to be the mighty spiritual warrior he has become or to be as blessed as he is in the Kingdom of God. Yet, one day when Billy Graham receives his reward from the Lord, a portion of that reward will be his mother's as well. Her investment of time, love, teaching, upbringing, feeding, and everything else she did for him, was an investment that will one day pay great dividends from the Lord. I am sure she did not use that as an incentive or motive in bringing up Billy, but nonetheless, it is a fact. We reap that which we sow, and that includes sowing into people.

Do not minimize the importance of loving. Love is the greatest of all attributes of the Holy Spirit.

1 Corinthians 13:3 NKJV
"And though I bestow all my goods to feed the poor, and though I give my body to be burned, but have not love, it profits me nothing."

God wants to use you for a very specific purpose. Understand, however, that these gifts, calling, visions, words of wisdom, and insights are not meant for you alone; they must be shared with others. Like the feeding of the five thousand, we need to partake, then pass it on to see miracles happen and to see God's glory firsthand. Then we must praise His holy name forever for His goodness and mercy.

As God roams the vast domain of the universe, does He really see us? Does He really care about the minute details of our lives? Are we really that important to Him?

Oh, yes, my friend, very much so. The question is not, "Can God still do miracles?" but rather, "How many unseen miracles has God done (and is doing daily) which we do not see or hear about?"

How about all the traffic delays God puts in our path so that we are not involved in some accident ahead of us? One day we will know, and be shocked to realize, the scores of times His love has protected us during our earthbound journey.

2 Chronicles 16:9

"For the eyes of the Lord run to and fro throughout the whole earth, to shew himself strong in the behalf of them whose heart is perfect toward him."

THE KING AWAITS
Philippians 3:20

THE GOD ROOM

8
Personal TUTORING

As I spent more time on my back porch in my God Room, I began learning deeper spiritual lessons from the Lord almost daily. Each one seemed to bring me closer to Him, closer to knowing the One who loved me even before I loved Him.

Each day was like a private tutoring lesson from the Master. I began to recognize His voice in contrast to my own voice speaking in my head. I would get my morning cup of coffee and head out to my back porch God Room to see what God had in store for me that day. It became a ritual and I looked forward to it, just me and God. No phones, no kids, no dog or cats, nothing to distract me from being alone quietly with Him.

Almost every day the Lord had something new for me to see. He was either teaching me a wonderful new concept or perhaps how to understand His ways a bit better, or even how to grasp those things I may have been a bit fuzzy about when reading His Word. Ususally it was learning through illustrations, like the parables in the Bible, showing me the Word's meaning through simple everyday surroundings, however unlike regular parables these lessons were in real life.

As I sat there He would have me look deeper with my spiritual eyes, not my natural eyes. Then He would explain to me what was really taking place.

It still astounds me how eager God is for us to know His ways, even to the smallest detail, if we follow His guidance. The Lord, through the Holy Spirit, has gently and patiently opened my spiritual eyes to see all that God has placed before me. His private tutoring in the God Room was and is like reading a 3-D Bible in real time action.

I had no idea God would take such time with me on a personal level until I began my quiet alone time with Him daily. In these special meetings, I was not accompanied by my wife, nor was she accompanied by me. Each born again, Spirit-filled believer is a child of the King, and amazingly, this Ruler of such a vast universe wants simple time with you alone.

Our God Rooms are all uniquely different. Most of the time I have my alone time with God (my God Room) on the back porch or sometimes driving alone in the car for a long distance. My wife likes to spend her quiet alone time with the Lord while she is still in bed. Either way seems to be fine with God as long as it is a quiet alone time where He is the main focus. Sometimes when I go out to my God Room on the back porch, we (God and I) never say a word, we just share that peaceful time alone in His comforting embrace, just like old friends; I love that too.

I would like to share some of my God Room experiences with you now.

Feeding THE FISH

Personal Tutoring

Within a short span of time, I saw how God, the great Creator, formed a small, unique ecosystem right before my eyes. During the previous two months, Florida had been going through a severe drought. Usually that time of year we experienced afternoon showers daily, which kept things green and replenished. However, during those couple of months we had nothing but sunshine. Although everyone enjoyed that perfect Florida weather, it was driving us slowly into a drought.

Usually, I was the one who did most of the listening in my back porch God Room. From my third-story condo, I could observe a small pond generally teeming with wildlife, which ranges from fish to ducks, snake birds (Anhinga) and cranes.

As the months passed, the pond continued to get smaller and smaller from the drought. Sometimes in my morning conversations with God, I would comment on it and ask the Lord if He could send some rain to keep the pond green and pristine. Fortunately, He is in control and not me, and my request was denied.

Daily I noticed how the water levels dropped from one foot, to two feet, to even three feet below where it should be. Consequently, as the water level continued to drop, many weeds and a lot of vegetation began to sprout up in those areas where the waterline used to be.

It was not the perfect pristine pond I once enjoyed. Even many of the birds were moving elsewhere to feed. It was almost as if God was neglecting this once perfect-looking pond by letting this growth of weeds take over.

When it finally began to rain, that little ecosystem appeared to be in grave danger. It was not just the normal afternoon Floridian shower; it seemed like the rain would never cease. A tropical depression was hovering over Florida, dumping inches of rain and raising the water level in the area almost to the point of flooding. Actually, in many outlying areas, it was flooding and creating problems for many people.

My wife and I commented a number of times on how high the water level was. You could see the tall vegetation growing along the shoreline sinking beneath the new water level at the pond, almost making a small marshland.

During one of my morning coffee sessions with the Lord, I mentioned how the pond had changed with the drought and then, the flood (just small talk sharing and bonding with God). I heard the Lord say to me, "Tell me what you see."

I surveyed the land and responded, "Well, the water level is somewhat higher than usual, and there are weeds growing

> **THE MEEK SHALL INHERIT**
> Matthew 5:5

in certain areas along the edges now. It is almost like a small marsh."

Like a father speaking to a small child with his hand outstretched and his finger pointing toward the pond, the Lord said softly, "I have fed the fish."

I began to see what God had been doing the whole time. I was content with my little pond environment all manicured and pristine. However, since I was not God, I could not see or know that under that water, the food supply for the fish was running low. God doesn't have a giant shaker filled with organic fish food like we use in our fish tanks at home. He does everything naturally and perfectly without chemicals or additives. In order to do that, sometimes God has to change the condition of things for many to preserve life for a few.

God orchestrated the drought in order that the plant life would take root along the shoreline, providing enough vegetation for the fish. Then the Lord sent the rain to refill the pond. He was not only feeding the fish, but in doing so, He was also taking care of the birds that fed on the fish, as well as creating a new habitat for the ducks, butterflies, and other creatures living on the pond. They were God's tenants in His natural habitat, and this loving "Landlord" cared for every one of them, rent free with provisions included.

In spite of my small complaints to the Lord about not keeping the pond as it was, I witnessed how God takes care of His own. He is the magnificent "Caretaker," not just of the environment, but also all the inhabitants of this planet.

FEEDING THE FISH

Along with being a loving God, fortunately, He is also a patient God who deals with my ignorance. I wonder if the angels pestered God when He was creating this world and said to Him, "God, you missed a spot over here." I think not. I dare say we are the only species who are arrogant enough to voice our opinions on matters that we know little or nothing about. With the suggestions we give God daily, along with the bickering and complaining, it is a wonder we don't hear a loud voice from heaven shouting, "Quiet! I've got this!"

Adam and Eve were given this world. God told them they had dominion over everything. It was theirs to manage and care for, but they signed over their ownership papers to Satan when they partook of the forbidden fruit. Now Satan is the rightful owner (see 2 Corinthians 4:4). It is rightfully his (for the time being). It's much like thousands of years ago when Esau sold his birthright to Jacob for a mere bowl of soup (see Genesis 25:34). Adam and Eve also sold (gave away) their inheritance to Satan for a piece of fruit off the tree.

The good news is, even though we acted dumber than any animal walking this earth by turning over full ownership to Satan, God never turned His back and said, "Well, there you go. You got what you deserved. Good luck now. See ya."

God kept this planet going (like He did with my pond), getting us out of the mess Adam created long ago. He did that by sending His only Son, Jesus Christ, and thereby giving those who believe a way out of the drought-like conditions into fertile land once again.

How many times has God made lemonade out of the lemons we have given Him? Not only has He been patient in the past, with the disobedient nation of Israel and the lost and hopeless Gentile world; He is also patiently engaged in our personal lives today. God is a master at that. Even when we are not looking, He still takes care of our needs. The birds know this, the fish know this, all the animals know this . . . except mankind. Blessed are those who do. We still have a tendency to question some of the actions God is taking in our lives. I truly believe there will be an era in heaven when God will sit down with us and explain all the times when He bailed us out of potential horrors; times when we never knew what was happening, and times when He saved us from scores of disasters we were oblivious to.

Even though God has us in the palm of His hand and cares for our needs, (see Philippians 4:19) still, we whine and complain. We spend much of our time and effort in securing our comfort so that we can store up for a rainy day; then we ask God not to change anything.

Even nature shows us that non-moving water becomes stagnant, undrinkable and even poisonous, if left in that state long enough. In contrast, water that comes from the top of the mountains has its impurities removed. It becomes pure, clean and usable by smashing against the stones and sometimes being driven underground with great pressure. So it is also with our lives. It is wise to become frugal, but we must be cautious because if we become too complacent, God will remove that impurity from us with hardships and loss. God is a loving God, but He is also a caring God as well. He does all things in our behalf and for our good.

Sometimes when we face difficulties, we ask God why doesn't He do something. Or we ask why He allowed those things to happen to us. We usually fail to realize that those times of being spiritually "smashed against the rocks" and "forced underground" also cause us to come out pure, clean and useful to the Lord.

Perhaps we need to have more humility like the so-called "dumb animals" who trust in the Lord so much they never question the world or storms around them; they simply trust and wait. I have never seen a cow that was left out in the field having a nervous breakdown because of the rain hitting its back and lightning striking all around it. The cow simply waits until it passes and then presses on. She may be wet, but she doesn't need pills or years of therapy to get on with her life afterward.

Indeed, having the "gift of knowledge" from that tree of knowledge was not a good thing as God declared thousands of years ago. He told Adam and Eve not to partake of it. Our "intellect and vast knowledge" have brought us to where we are today, a society of deaf ears and blind eyes.

The Bible tells us not to fear that which we can see but fear what we cannot see. What we can see may take our life, but that which we cannot see may take our very soul if we are not careful and stay close to the Lord. Trust in the Lord. As Job so brilliantly said (quoted on page 63 as well), *"Though He slay me, yet will I trust in Him."*

We need to wise up and be dumb cows! I don't really believe God wants this though, because He gave us dominion over all things in this earth, and with that, came responsibility. It would be a far different world to live in today had we never known of "good and evil," which resulted from eating that fruit. I have often wondered what this world would have been like if Adam and Eve had not partaken and we lived free from evil. I guess one day we will find out, during the Millennium, the thousand-year reign of Christ (see Revelation 20:4).

Until that time, we must try and make lemonade out of the lemons the world hands us or by the things we bring on ourselves. We do that, not by relying on our own understanding, but by leaning on His wisdom and understanding (see Proverbs 3:5-6). We must let go and let God direct our steps.

I heard a cute story many years ago about a young child and a village toymaker. The child had a broken toy and brought it to the toymaker for repairs. He knew the toymaker was excellent at repairing broken things and was excited about bringing his broken toy to be repaired.

As the little boy came into the shop, he began telling the toymaker all that was wrong with the toy. After a long explanation, the toymaker smiled at the boy and reached out for the toy to repair it. As he did, the boy pulled the toy back and started pointing out others things wrong with it as well. When the boy was finished, the toymaker once again reached out to take the toy to repair it.

A CHILD'S PRAYER
Revelation 8:3-4

Once again, the boy pulled it back, pointing out still more areas he felt needed work. This went on a number of times until finally the toymaker reached out, took the toy from the little boy, and gently said, "Young man, I cannot fix it if you will not let it go."

So it is with many of us. We bring our broken lives before the Lord for repair, telling God all the details but we, too, must let go. We cannot have God start to do a little bit and say to Him, "OK, God, I got it from here, thanks." If we turn our lives and problems over to God, we need to let go completely, trusting in the fact that He made all things, so He can also fix all things. What better hands to be in than the ones that made all things to begin with! Like the old saying, "There is nothing more dangerous than a man with a little bit of knowledge. Leave it with the Master."

God may have to put us through some dry times, but if so, it is only to flood our lives with blessings once the ground is fully ready to yield fruit once again.

John 10:10 NKJV

"I have come that they may have life, and that they may have it more abundantly."

I found an interesting verse in the Bible I want to share with you. I never fully understood its meaning until the Holy Spirit revealed it to me during my alone time with the Lord.

2 Corinthians 8:15 NKJV

As it is written, "He who gathered much had nothing left over, and he who gathered little had no lack."

This verse came to me one morning and I did not understand the message behind it; however, I could not take my eyes or thoughts away from it. When I asked the Holy Spirit to please explain its meaning so that I could understand it better, He did.

In Matthew 17:24-27, being confronted by taxpayers, Jesus told Peter to throw out a hook, no bait, just a hook. Immediately, Peter caught a fish with a shiny coin in its mouth, which was just enough to pay the taxes for Jesus and Peter. Coincidence? No, God-incidence! God put that scenario together to glorify His Son who trusted His Father in all things. Jesus performed the miracle as needed.

Some may indeed be blessed more in finances than others; however, God has instructed those with more to also give more to the poor and tithe accordingly, in order to share the abundant blessings with others. As the above Bible verse commands, those who have more than they need should give to the less fortunate, so that those who have less will also be filled. It is yet another step in becoming more like Christ.

2 Corinthians 8:9 NKJV

"For you know the grace of our Lord Jesus Christ, that though He was rich, yet for your sakes He became poor, in order that you through His poverty might become rich."

This sharing of wealth does not apply only to financial riches. The same principle holds true with the riches of wisdom and grace God has granted. "To whom much is given, much is required" (see Luke 12:48). God's ways are far more precious than money or jewels could ever be, and they can never be taken from you.

Wisdom and grace may indeed be the only riches you possess that you can take with you when you leave here. However,

FEEDING THE FISH

your reward in heaven may not be as much if you do not share that wisdom and grace with others. Anything given to you by God is always meant to be shared in order to multiply from one to another, just like the feeding of the five thousand. It started out with a few fish and a couple of loaves of bread. Because it was commanded to be shared and passed on one to another, it multiplied enough to feed the five thousand and more was left over.

God is a fair judge, in all matters, yet as the bible often says, God does not think like man does and sometimes it is hard for us to understand His ways because we use our logic to understand His. Even in our own court system, if we win the case we get that which we ask for, no more and no less. (Within the judgement of the court) However in God's court, we receive what is the best, not necessarily what we ask for in compensation. God sees all things in the "big picture" and our due reward is set to such.

Let me illustrate by using myself as an example. Say I bring my case of finances before God's courtroom and declare, "Lord. I am barely making ends meet, although my work is everywhere and other people are making much money off the work I have done. I therefore humbly ask for just compensation to these regards."

The Lord will consider the plea/charge and make His decision. He may say, "Granted" and slam down the hammer, yet my finances may not change at all. What I asked for ($) did not come to past in my mind, but in fact I was granted "much" in a far better way. In God's eyes He knows that money is not a suitable reward. Money comes and goes, and is only good down here for the short time we are here. Yet by withholding money, my life (through

struggling yet relying on Him) continues to build character, and character is something of true value. Value that I will be able to reap from that investment throughout all of eternity.

Now take this mind set, and apply it to the bible verse: "The one who gathered much, did not have too much." meaning the one who had a lot of anything (money, wealth, possessions) did not have much regarding things in the spiritual realm. You cannot take them with you and most of our life will be spent in heaven, not here.

However, "the one who gathered little did not have too little." By not being reliant on our own wealth (having little) yet reliant on God for our needs, this person was rich in character and integrity. Something that will only gain "interest" in that investment as time continues on, even after this life is over and done. Indeed that person did not have "too little" for God does supply all our needs, not wants perhaps, but our needs. If our needs are met, then we do not have "too little", and in the long term (the big picture) we shall gain far more in the end then he who had gathered much down here.

If we are to know God we need to change our way of thinking to be more like His, in the "big picture" of things. By knowing Him better this way, we can understand Him better in what He is doing in our lives.

God is a God of equality. He does not love one more than another, nor does He care for one more than another. Some of us may indeed receive more giftings than others, but we all are given opportunities to receive rewards from those giftings God gives us. It is up to us to take advantage of those opportunities and blessings by following the Lord's guidance and wisdom closely.

Now when we look at the verse in

2 Corinthians 8:15, we see, indeed, the one who gathered much did not have too much (money is nothing) but the one who gathered little did not have too little, for strong character and solid integrity is no little gain by any means.

The bottom line here is to trust God to supply your needs. People hold back finances because they want some leftovers in reserve; in doing so, they make themselves the supplier of their own needs. If the people of the world would live as God commanded, there is enough money and jewels so that none would go hungry; none would be living on the streets, and everyone would be taken care of. This world does not know God or depend on Him for their needs. By depending on themselves, the end result is that the world will always be needy.

Like Jesus said, "The poor you have with you always" (John 12:8 NKJV). He said that because He knew the heart of man without God.

Luke 6:38
"Give, and it shall be given unto you; good measure, pressed down, and shaken together, and running over, shall men give into your bosom. For with the same measure that ye mete withal it shall be measured to you again."

We do not follow this to enhance our wealth, but we follow this because our King has so decreed it to be so. He promised that, and God cannot break His promises.

One more thing the Lord showed me in regards to His feeding of the fish while I was with Him in my God Room was chaos and cosmos. The antonym for the word

FEEDING THE FISH

chaos is cosmos, and this word can mean "order," or it can also mean "universe." How can cosmos mean both order and universe? Because there was order in the universe that God created. So when all things are functioning as they are supposed to, all is according to God's will and His blessing. When God created all things in the universe one by one, chaos subsided and order and stability came into creation.

Such is the case regarding the moon. After going there, our astronauts found the moon devoid of life. It is primarily just rocks and dust. However, that seemingly "useless" part of creation has a very valuable role in our lives because of the rise and fall of the tides.

While tides involve the vertical movement of water, currents are horizontal movements. People who live on the sea or near it need to understand currents, tides, and wave motions. This knowledge is invaluable to them. Sailors can ride out storms on high seas without losing control of their boats if they know how to handle their vessels in storms. Many land and aquatic creatures take advantage of daily tidal activity. Many animals and plants use the movement of the tides to carry them between breeding areas in protected estuaries, and then back out to deeper ocean waters.

Land animals also take advantage of the plants and immobile organisms revealed by receding tides as food sources. Sometimes fish and small aquatic animals will become trapped in small pools of water left behind by the low tides, making easy meals for seabirds. The removal of large quantities of water also helps to recirculate shoreline nutrients and help dilute and remove any pollutants that would otherwise accumulate along the shore.

Just as God allowed the dry spell to feed the fish at the pond by making waves at sea, God can feed the larger numbers of fish in the ocean, which in turn feed us. Sometimes hardships must come to pass in order for life to prevail.

In the order of the cosmos, God does all the work. The only thing that is expected of us is to trust and believe in His love and caring nature during any hardships. This is such an easy task, yet in the midst of calamity, it can be the hardest to achieve.

We need more than just reading a passage or two on a daily basis; we need God's Word penetrating us to the deepest core of our being.

Recently I saw a minister put a bag of aspirin on her head and ask, "Do you think this aspirin will get rid of my headache like this?"

Just skimming over or reading it daily does little, if anything, for our spiritual growth. We have to take in that Word, digest it, let it filter throughout our being for it to work within our spirits. Even a small piece of one aspirin will do far more digested, than a bag of aspirin merely on our heads.

John 14:27 NIV
"Peace I leave with you; my peace I give you. I do not give to you as the world gives. Do not let your hearts be troubled and do not be afraid."

John 16:33 NIV
"I have told you these things, so that in me you may have peace. In this world you will have trouble. But take heart! I have overcome the world."

THE TRINITY
John 1:1-5

Matthew 24:6-8 NIV

"You will hear of wars and rumors of wars, but see to it that you are not alarmed. Such things must happen, but the end is still to come. Nation will rise against nation, and kingdom against kingdom. There will be famines and earthquakes in various places. All these are the beginning of birth pains."

I assume there may be many non-believers who might read this and say, "Peace? You tell us all these calamities and then declare you give us peace?!" To the world, that indeed may sound contrary, but that is because they do not have the counsel of the Holy Spirit in them. It is not a matter of intellect, but a matter of spiritual guidance that brings forth the light and the truth.

It's like small children who run to their mother or father frightened and crying in fear when they see a flash of lightning and hear the thunder around them. It is the peace within that enables parents to console their children and hold them close, whispering, "It's all right." The solid, unshakable peace of the parents will calm their children and let them know there is peace in the midst of the storm. The children feel the peace through their parents' confidence and the unshakable trust that they will protect them.

We are God's children. He has told us of things to come and then He holds us close and whispers, "It is OK. I have overcome the world. My peace I give unto you" (see John 14:27 NIV).

Trust and pray, dear, sweet child of the King. Know that the prayers of the righteous avail much before the King who is in control and loves us beyond comprehension. When we pray, God listens. However, when we put faith behind those prayers, we see God move!

It is one thing to know the Word of God in our minds, but quite another thing to actually know the Word of God in our heart of hearts. If we have a memorized verses from the Word, we may impress others, but when we place that Word in our heart of hearts, and digest it into our inner being, then that "knowing" impresses God and He draws close to us.

James 4:8

"Draw nigh to God, and he will draw nigh to you."

Let me illustrate further. Diana is my wife. People may say, "I know Diana," and that is fine, because many people do. But when I, as her husband say, "I know Diana," then it takes on a different, fuller meaning. It is not just knowing that she exists, but knowing her intimately and deeply as one who is with her every day. That *knowing* is totally different. The Lord wants us to have that same type of knowing.

2 Timothy 2:15

"Study to shew thyself approved unto God."

The Lord commands this in His Word. This does not mean to study the Word just to memorize verses, but to study and dig deeply to know its full meaning.

Once it is within us, we can never forget. Like a well of spring water whenever we are thirsty, the Word flows upward. It is from that spring, that our power in Christ will be manifested. It is imperative that you know who you are in Christ.
who you are in Christ Jesus.

> ### WORD OF GOD
> Matthew 24:35

FEEDING THE FISH

Personal Tutoring

John 6:47

"Verily, verily, I say unto you, He that believeth on me hath everlasting life."

We who are Christians know this verse very well. It is our salvation and hope that we shall never die. We will be with the Lord forever! What a great and magnificent gift from God! This assurance is based on His grace, not on what we deserve or have done. However, many Christians who have taken that step of faith sadly stop there. They are now assured of their salvation and a place in heaven by believing in Jesus, and standing on the promise of God. Alas, they have their "Golden Ticket" to ride that great salvation train into heaven, but they never progress.

Acts 16:31 NKJV

"Believe on the Lord Jesus Christ, and you will be saved."

God's gift has so much more to offer then just a place in heaven. Eternal life is both quantitative and qualitative. Eternal life (everlasting life) has both a quantitative aspect (lasting forever) and also a qualitative aspect (growing in fullness). There is more to God's gift then just longevity; there is also an added aspect of quality of life if we walk

> **GOLDEN TICKET**
> Hebrews 4:16

with Him daily. Jesus stated this many times and ways.

John 10:10 NKJV

"That you may have life, and, have it more abundantly."

John 14:6

"I am the way, the truth, and the life."

John 11:25

"I am the resurrection, and the life."

Having eternal life and knowing that these years on earth are not the end, are gifts from God, for which we should forever be grateful. God loved us that much that He gave His only Son to pay the supreme price for our souls. Sadly, what so many don't realize is that God not only gave us an opportunity for eternal life with Him in heaven, He also offers an opportunity for a better life while we are still down here, a double gift! The second part, however, does require serious effort and dedication on our part, a daily walk with Him.

I heard a minister one time suggest that Christians who only accept the Lord but never bother to live their lives by walking each day with Him are no better than robbers and thieves. In believing that Jesus is the Son of God, they receive their golden ticket to board heaven's "train"; however, they continue to live pretty much as they want. Basically they take the gift God offers through His grace and say, "Thank you very much," and go on their way without so much as a handshake.

I don't know that I necessarily agree with that pastor's point of view completely, but I can tell you this: To receive God's gift of salvation, and then refuse to walk daily with the Lord, is a very precarious way to live.

God will not go back on His promises. He never has; He never will. God said "Believe on the Lord Jesus Christ and thou shalt be saved" (Acts 16:31). God declared in His Word, and so it shall be. However, we have to understand the character of God. He does not merely give us an invitation to join Him in heaven; He wants to make our lives better now!

In accepting the Lord as your Savior, you must surrender your heart, not just because you want that golden ticket or because it sounds like a good idea (acceptance from your mind). Let me explain what I mean by a firsthand encounter I have experienced.

I knew a person who was a devoted "New Age" believer. She and I had known each other quite well for a number of years, and we talked many times about Jesus and the importance of accepting Him into one's life. Her point of view was that Jesus was a good man and a wonderful teacher. That is true on both accounts, but in spite of all our lengthy conversations, she could not bring herself to believe that Jesus was the only begotten Son of God or that He is the only way to heaven.

One day she looked me in the eye and told me that the previous night she had accepted the Lord into her heart. I was shocked. I was even more shocked with regards to my complacency over her announcement. I did not feel overjoyed for her as I should have,

and that deeply troubled me. I should have been ecstatic, jumping up and down with her. Yet, neither of us rejoiced. I smiled, hugged her and told her how happy I was for her, but deep inside I was puzzled by my lack of emotion and joy. I could sense a look on her face that told me she, too, expected something more inside that perhaps was missing.

As time went on, I saw no change in her at all. She still attended her New Age church and even invited me to attend one Sunday with her. Since I had never attended one, I accepted. I sat through the service, which was very nice and filled with loving people. I even heard the preacher mention Jesus a couple times, but it was the same old "Good-man-and-wonderful-teacher" tag they applied when talking about Him. After the service, with a broad smile on her face, she was eager to know what I thought about her church.

I remember looking into her eyes to get her full attention and said, "This church is the most dangerous place I have ever been, and I am a Vietnam war veteran."

2 Timothy 3:5
"Having a form of godliness, but denying the power thereof: from such turn away."

Establishments like this (and not just the New Age churches alone) have fooled thousands of people into believing they already have that golden ticket. These poor souls will never seek Christ for their salvation. Why would they? Those so-called churches have told them they already have it. They are accepted as they are, so why go to Jesus for something they already have? Unfortunately, those deluded people will never know the truth until it is too late.

Satan has planted that lie deep within their hearts, and not just that particular deception, but many false related beliefs. There are many wrong ideas spiritually contaminating this world. Just like thousands of years ago when the devil told Eve, "You will not surely die" (Genesis 3:4 NKJV). From that very second, both of them did die spiritually and began dying physically. Adam and Eve were meant to live forever with God, walking with Him every day. After they took a bite of that fruit, their bodies began to die, not immediately, but they died nonetheless. More importantly, their spirits died instantly. Satan continues to tell that lie to anyone who will believe it. Non-believers may accept that we all die physically, but often refuse to believe that we have all died spiritually until it is too late.

So why then did my New Age friend say the words of salvation when accepting the Lord if she never really repented and purposed to follow Christ? The real attitude she had in that moment is only known to her and God, but from the evidence before me, I would have to say she just wanted to cover herself. Perhaps she thought by saying the words like some kind of "Abracadabra," she would be safe one day when she died because she had her golden ticket in hand. I am dumfounded by people who think they can fool God, for He sees our hearts, not just our actions or mere words. God is not a man that He can be fooled, and God doesn't deal with "magic words."

Luke 8:12

"Those by the way side are they that hear; then cometh the devil, and taketh away the word out of their hearts, lest they should believe and be saved."

Our plea for salvation and our acceptance of the Lord's gift come only from the heart. God hears our hearts far more than our words or thoughts. Although God made our physical bodies from the earth's dust, He uniquely designed mankind's inner being as spirit after His own image. It is by our spirit that we reach God, not by our bodies or our minds. When you pray, if you simply say the words from your mouth, they will fall to the ground. When our spirit cries out, God truly hears. This is why Jesus said to the Samaritan woman:

John 4:24

"God is a Spirit: and they that worship him must worship him in spirit and in truth."

Accepting the Lord as our Savior and Deliverer from hell must come from our innermost being, and it must be done in truth. Trying Jesus out for a while will not work. We must have a spiritual and soulful experience based on truth before God, or we are experiencing a ritual that will trick our minds into thinking the mission is accomplished and we have gained the ticket.

Even when individuals come to the Lord and accept Jesus Christ as their Savior, that is only the quantitative part of the offer God has granted. The qualitative part of God's gift can minister to us now, not just in the hereafter.

The Lord does not just wish us to have an eternal life alone (quantitative) but also to have a life filled with the fruits of the Spirit (qualitative). Christ died and rose again that we might have both.

God has many hidden treasures for us along our life's journey, but if we do not take the time to listen to God's instructions,

we will miss many of them and our lives will not be as complete as the Lord intends. He made us unique individuals, not only in our bodies, minds, and spirits, but also in that which we accomplish for His Kingdom. We are the body of Christ. Some are hands, some feet, some eyes, and so on. Each has a unique purpose and plan that all fit together to make up His body, the church.

The church (God's people) is not a building or a denomination; it is the bride of Christ, a title for God's people mentioned only a few times in Scripture (see Revelations 19:7-9 and Ephesians 5:25-27). As God ordained the husband and wife to be one, so also should we (the bride) become one with Christ Himself. An old saying declares, "Sometimes we are the only Christ that others will see." Those are not mere words. We are to do Christ's bidding as Jesus did His Father's bidding when He was here on earth.

This need not be a cumbersome duty or task, for Jesus said, "Come to Me, all who are weary and heavy laden, and I will give you rest. Take My yoke upon you..." (Matthew 11:28 NKJV).

If we are truly one with Christ, then whatever we throw upon our spiritual backs is also on Christ's back, and Jesus never grows weary of the load. How do we do this? By having an intimate relationship with the Lord. We can be so close that nothing can separate us from His love. How do you obtain this close relationship with God? By spending quality alone time with Him in your God Room.

I often find this interesting. Surveys reveal that when people are asked what they want in life, most desire complete peace. Jesus is the Prince of peace. He has proven that to us time and time again, especially by calming a raging sea, a dangerous dilemma that was terrifying even for well-seasoned sailors.

Jesus was so filled with peace that His words alone calmed that sea immediately and made the disciples gasp in awe.

Others may say riches will make them completely happy and comforted. Why? What do riches do to enhance life? It may pay all the bills, but will it give them comfort in their souls, or insure their health? Those things are only provided through Christ, at least for those who follow Him closely. The Lord supplies all our needs.

Philippians 4:19

"My God shall supply all your need according to his riches in glory by Christ Jesus."

You may want a new Cadillac, but in reality, all you need is a reliable way to get around. You may want lots of money in the bank so you will feel secure if disaster strikes, but really, all you need is to know that your needs will be met on a daily basis. You may *want* an attractive, flashy woman by your side, but what you *need* is a good God-fearing woman who is beautiful within, to help you in your walk.

Whenever I try to understand more about the God I worship, I look at it from the vantage point of a father/child relationship. I want the very best for my kids, but I will not sacrifice their character and integrity for things they simply want. Spoiling a child, at any age, is never good or productive. Indeed, it robs them of many things they will need in the future. If we sincerely care about our children, we want the best for them;

MY PRAYER
Matthew 14:19

however, the best for them builds character on the inside.

I knew a man whose son seemed to have a hard time making ends meet on a regular basis. The father tried to help him in any way he could, which usually ended up being financial. Although the young man accepted the Lord in his heart, he did not truly make Him Lord of his life. He was a good person at heart, which is why it was hard for that father to ignore his pleas.

One day he had a large utility bill that accumulated from non-payments. The boy told his father they were going to cut off his electric and water if he did not pay the bill. The father delayed as long as he could, hoping his son would get the money himself. The father was ready to bail him out of this large financial hole when he heard from God distinctly, "Stop! You're getting in My way!"

Needless to say, he was a bit taken back by this, but understood what the Lord was saying. If he came to his rescue, his son would learn to rely on his dad, not God. Unknowingly, this father was replacing God in his son's life. His son needed to seek God as his supplier. As long as Dad was in that intermediate role, God could never show Him what He could and would do for him.

His dad did not come to the rescue that particular time, and his son did finally make ends meet. It helped to establish a solid and responsible work ethic within that young lad, and today he has a steady job. The Lord opened a door for him which suited his talents perfectly. I pray he will never forget where his *real* resources come from.

I am not saying that we should not help one another and should throw it all on God's lap. But if we stay sensitive to the Holy Spirit and spend quality alone time with God, He will guide us in what needs to be done for God's will to be accomplished.

Christ came that we might have life and have it more abundantly, including eternal life with the Father that never ends. However, Jesus also came that we may have life abundantly now. If we only grab the golden ticket, we miss out on so much more the Lord has for us in life, both here and hereafter. Remember, all we do or do not do for Christ is recorded in the books. God has much in this life He wants you and me to accomplish for our glory one day in heaven. With one Word from His mouth, God could make all things right instantaneously, but if He did that, we would not have the opportunity to share the victorious everlasting glory with Him in heaven.

I hope and pray that most of you reading this can say, "Yes, I know all this already." If so, then you have both stubs to that ticket, both parts of God's gift. Have you accepted and found that the Lord is good in all that He does? Remember, God is our Father, and like any father who wants his child to have a nice home, He also wants the child to be happy, too. We have secured our nice home (mansion in the sky), so let us also receive the happiness and peace in our lives today by our relationship with Him.

John 17:3 NKJV
"And this is eternal life, that they may know You, the only true God, and Jesus Christ whom You have sent."

2 Peter 3:18 NIV
"But grow in the grace and knowledge of our Lord and Savior Jesus Christ."

The gift of life is a gift freely given to all. We may conclude that because it is freely given, it is therefore free. It is not. It costs dearly. Not only will it cost you everything you have, but also everything you are. God says I not only want all you have but I want your very life as well. Anything less is short of the full payment required for eternal life, which Christ provided at His resurrection.

Remember the story of Jesus and the rich man?

Mark 10:20-21 NLT
"Teacher," the man replied, "I've obeyed all these commandments since I was young." Looking at the man, Jesus felt genuine love for him. "There is still one thing you haven't done," he told him. "Go and sell all your possessions and give the money to the poor, and you will have treasure in heaven. Then come, follow me."

Unfortunately, the rich man walked away sad because he had much and was not willing to give it up. However, I want to point one other hidden aspect of this story we tend to overlook. Jesus told the man, not only to give up what he had, but to follow Him. In other words, He was urging the rich man not to go back to his old way of living, but instead, to give up his former life and begin patterning his life after Jesus. God wants it all, your possessions and your life as well. It has to all be His if you are to be a disciple of Christ.

The gift of eternal life is not free; it will cost you dearly, but is it worth it? Oh, yes, even to those who do not believe would say yes if they were guaranteed eternal life. Who among them would not give everything they have to be granted a never-ending life? Yet, "payment in full" cannot be stamped on them until they turn over all their possessions, including their very lives. The demand is undying love, praise, and total commitment to the Lord Jesus Christ, wanting nothing but Him.

Harsh payment? Unrealistic to achieve? Yes, if based only on our own strength, our own

ability to pay. We must have God's grace to fulfill such a demand. And that grace came through the Lord's sacrifice. That is exactly why Jesus had to pay that price for us. Eternal life, that golden ticket, is not free by any means, and no man or woman can afford such a high fee to obtain it. But Christ paid that entrance fee and gave it to us as a gift of His love. All we have to do is believe on Him and believe that He is the only begotten Son of the living God, and it is ours.

If you do not know Jesus Christ as your Savior, pray this simple prayer to receive Him now:

Dear God, I know I'm a sinner, I know I am not where I want to be, and I need your forgiveness! Please wash me clean from all sin, shame, and guilt. I believe that Jesus died on the cross to pay the price for my sins and was resurrected again so I can have eternal life. Jesus come into my life to be my Lord and Savior. Guide my life and help me to do Your will. I thank You, Lord, and I believe that I shall spend all eternity with You from this day on. Amen!

If you have said those words out loud and believed them from your heart (not just from your head), then you, too, are now a child of the living God. You now share in the inheritance of Jesus Christ. We are no longer called His servants but His friends, His kin, for we are one with Christ Himself.

John 15:15 NKJV
"No longer do I call you servants, for a servant does not know what his master is doing; but I have called you friends, for all things that I heard from My Father I have made known to you."

Personal Tutoring

As I have said many times before, "We can never out-give God." So then what have we given the Lord to be one with Him and granted eternal life with the Lord forever and ever? That brings me to the next part of this message I received from the Lord in my God Room: You can take it with you.

We have always been told that when we die, we cannot take our possessions with us. The world even laughs at that saying, though inside they are distraught, especially those who have acquired great wealth. However, I am here to say you CAN take it with you. Yes, you can indeed take all your wealth and earnings with you, but not those in the form of gold coins, paper money, or material investments. The investments of which I am speaking are "jewels" of a spiritual nature.

Throughout our life we accumulate spiritual wealth of gems and precious jewels in the form of character, integrity, and refinement of soul. These are the treasures Christ talks about when He mentions treasures that do not rust or cannot be taken by a thief.

Remember where you're going when you leave here. Will gold coins, stocks and bonds do you any good in heaven? Is not everything yours for the asking there? If so, then there is no need for stores and no

place to spend your money. One of your greatest assets now is knowing who you are in Christ, your position in the family of God, and what your destiny is in the world to come.

Matthew 6:19-21 NKJV

"Do not lay up for yourselves treasures on earth, where moth and rust destroy and where thieves break in and steal; but lay up for yourselves treasures in heaven, where neither moth nor rust destroys and where thieves do not break in and steal. For where your treasure is, there your heart will be also."

Thieves can rob you of material wealth; governments can snatch your land and investments, but no one can rob or take away your integrity and character unless you give it to them. Who you are is worth far more than what you have in material wealth.

Why do people save? Perhaps it is the security of knowing that they will always have what they need. Does not the Lord promise this for those who follow Him?

Perhaps they store up their possessions for power. The Lord tells us because we are the sons of God that we have all the power of that title. No harm shall befall us, and no enemy shall overcome us.

Perhaps the world saves up wealth so their needs will be met if sickness comes their way. The Word of God promises us

> ### ASCENSION
> John 1:14

that we have the greatest physician of all time at our disposal 24/7. We have more wealth than anyone could ever hope for, and we can take all *that* wealth with us when we leave here. No thief can ever rob us, no government can ever snatch it from our hands, and it will never rust or decay. Our spiritual wealth is secure in the holdings of God Himself.

The bank we store all this in shall never go bankrupt or need financial assistance. There are no recessions or depressions in heaven; no tsunami waves to wash it away, and no fire to destroy what we have in the Lord Jesus Christ.

We can, indeed, take it all with us when we leave, and if we do the Lord's bidding by working hard for His glory down here, we may have a fleet of angels carry the cargo with us on our departure. The catch is, we have only a short time down here to accumulate that wealth. For only a few years, we have the opportunity to achieve what we shall possess and enjoy forever in heaven with the Lord.

Yes, Jesus paid the price that we can obtain our salvation (Golden Ticket), but the wealth we bring with us depends on our servitude to Him now. We shall reap what we sow, but the time is limited. We only have one lifetime, so use that time now and invest it wisely.

Matthew 25:14-29
"For the kingdom of heaven is as a man travelling into a far country, who called his own servants, and delivered unto them his goods. And unto one he gave five talents, to another two, and to another one; to every man according to his several ability; and straightway took his journey. Then he that had received the five talents went and traded with the same, and made them other five talents. And likewise he that had received two, he also gained other two. But he that had received one went and digged in the earth, and hid his lord's money. After a long time the lord of those servants cometh, and reckoneth with them. And so he that had received five talents came and brought other five talents, saying, Lord, thou deliveredst unto me five talents: behold, I have gained beside them five talents more. His lord said unto him, Well done, thou good and faithful servant: thou hast been faithful over a few things, I will make thee ruler over many things: enter thou into the joy of thy lord. He also that had received two talents came and said, Lord, thou deliveredst unto me two talents: behold, I have gained two other talents beside them. His lord said unto him, Well done, good and faithful servant; thou hast been faithful over a few things, I will make thee ruler over many things: enter thou into the joy of thy lord. Then he which had received the one talent came and said, Lord, I knew thee that thou art an hard man, reaping where thou hast not sown, and gathering where thou hast not strawed: And I was afraid, and went and hid thy talent in the earth: lo, there thou hast that is thine. His lord answered and said unto him, Thou wicked and slothful servant, thou knewest that I reap where I sowed not, and gather where I have not strawed: Thou oughtest therefore to have put my money to the exchangers, and then at my coming I should have received mine own with usury. Take therefore the talent from him, and give it unto him which hath ten talents. For unto every one that hath shall be given, and he shall have abundance: but from him that hath not shall be taken away even that which he hath."

RECEIVING
John 14:17

RAINBOWS

Personal Tutoring

& Reflections

The Bible says that God has instilled His Word in us, but it takes the Holy Spirit to open our eyes and ears that we can see and hear what God is communicating. This was one of those eye-opening experiences I received from the Lord as I spent time alone with Him.

From my back porch I noticed, in the distance, a large cloud starting to rain. Then I began to see a small rainbow appear. Nothing extraordinary happened: that's just how rainbows work (light filtering through the droplets of rain). However, I noticed it did not take the shape as usual. Instead of the arc across the sky, this rainbow was formed in the shape of the falling rain. It followed a path, waving in a vertical direction much like the rain mist. The odd form still had the normal color of a rainbow with highlights against the water droplets in the air. As I kept sipping my coffee and observing God's performance of colored light before me, I felt the Lord speak (in His quiet still voice inside me): "What do you see?"

I replied, "A beautiful rainbow, Lord. Thank You. What a great way to start the day." As I smiled to myself, thinking my verbal appreciation and compliments would score some points with Him, He said, "No, look closer . . . what do you really see?"

As I looked closer and watched this

> ## GOD'S PROMISE
> ### 2 Corinthians 1:20

rainbow grow larger by the minute, I started to realize what God was bringing to my attention: the majesty and the testament of His Son, Jesus Christ, presented in full, living color!

Rainbows are visual prisms. They include every color there is. To the naked eye, they are basically four distinct hues, red, yellow, green, and purple.

When I paint rainbows on canvas, I usually simulate those colors. I add red, yellow, green, and purple paint onto the canvas. Then I blend them all together and presto, a rainbow! As I studied these colors that made up the rainbow, I came to realize why God chose those particular four distinct colors as representation for His promise found in Genesis 9:12-17.

Red is the easiest and most obvious color to understand because it signifies the blood Christ shed for us on Calvary, washing away our sins. Next to that was yellow, and on either side of the yellow hue is red and green, which are used to tint (ever so slightly) the yellow to make that wonderful golden color. That signifies the most precious commodity we have down here, gold. So it fits right in because Christ is precious indeed. The next color we have is green. Even the kids today know that this color signifies life, and Christ is life, the only real life there is.

Last, but not least, is the color purple. Throughout the ages, purple has always signified royalty and majesty, which relates to Jesus, the King of kings and Lord of lords! Yes, it all fits together perfectly, a colorful, wondrous visualization of Christ in the sky.

Psalm 19:1 NIV
"The heavens declare the glory of God; the skies proclaim the work of his hands."

As I started my morning, I watched God shape this rainbow that was growing bigger and more brilliant as the rain kept falling, I also saw a bold testament of God's Son, Jesus Christ, right before my eyes across the sky.

The Lord also brought another point to mind. Being an artist, I knew about colors and the mixtures needed to achieve those desired colors. I also knew from other experiences outside of painting that there is a vast difference between colors of light and colors of pigment that I use when I paint.

When you mix all the colors of pigments together (in perfect and equal amounts), the result is black. However, quite the opposite is true regarding colors of light. If you project different colors onto a screen from different projectors aiming at one point, the merging colors of light become white. So combining the "earthly" colors gives you black, and all the "heavenly" colors from a light source give you white.

Conclusion? Because a rainbow is not made up from earthly pigmentations, it is comprised from different colors of light in specific order. If we were to put all the colors together from the rainbows, the result would be pure, white light, the representation of God Himself. The rainbow colors separately are different facets of Christ, but when put together, we get the Father.

Christ is all things to all people. He even has many names that accompany all the things that make up His nature. When we combine all that Jesus is, the result is the white pure concentrated light of the Father Himself. Interesting, huh?

So, as I lay back trying to take in all I learned for the day in my God Room, I thought my lesson was complete. I began thanking Him for the glorious day, what my eyes had seen and for loving me enough to share it with me in full color (pun intended). However, as I continued soaking it up, I began to see other things around my scenic view.

Because it was a peaceful, quiet day, the water reflection was almost perfectly still, like a mirror. You could see the clear reflection of the trees and condos on the water as if a huge mirror was placed on the ground before them. As I looked across the pond, I began to ask God why He made reflections, knowing there is a reason and purpose for everything. Once again, the Lord said, "Look at the reflections. Tell me what you see?"

"I see the trees, buildings, birds flying by and landing, disturbing the water as they come and go, and the reflections seem to be a mirror-image of those things. Also, the reflections become distorted at times if the water is disturbed by wind or movement in the waters."

The Lord patiently added, "Yes, now look with your spiritual eye, not just your natural ones. What do you see now?"

As I continued to observe the surroundings, I began connecting those visuals images with spiritual connotations, trying to see them as God sees them. It became apparent that the reflections before me were representations of life, only in duplicate form. There were the real objects (the artifacts), and then there were the reflections (a representation of those things) cast upon the waters.

RAINBOWS AND REFLECTIONS

When all is still, we see the reflection is in perfect alliance with what is actually there. When there is a disturbance, the waters are distorted and so is our perception of what is on the shore before us. If we only look at the reflection, we get a false illusion of the reality before us. Therefore, if a strong wind blows, we cannot see the reflections, or if a heavy fog rolls in, we might deduce that there is nothing at all on the shoreline. It does not mean the trees are not there; it simply means we cannot see them at that time, judging by the lack of reflections in the water.

Life is much like this. The devil goes to great effort to make duplications or replications of what God has already made. Then he distorts them so we cannot see clearly, and he tells us all is gone array, or he distorts them so much through his disturbances that when we take our eyes off the truth, all seems lost.

One image is the truth, the real tree standing there; the other (the reflection) is an imitation of that truth. Do we look up at the trees, or do we look at the reflection that is closer to us and judge what is on the shore? We live in this world, and sometimes the things around us seem closer than the God of the heavens. The Bible says He is closer than a brother (see Proverbs 18:24).

God answers prayers, always has, always will. Sometimes it's immediate, sometimes you have to wait a while, and then sometimes the answer is "No," but He will always answer your prayer. God is steadfast and dependable. When the winds and storms of this world blow against us, often we look at the water's reflection and ask, "God, where are the trees You promised?"

In our confusion and desperate state, we claim that God has removed them because we cannot see them; thus, we conclude God either did not hear us or He changed His mind. Neither is true. The trees are still there, but the reflection does not show them clearly anymore. Not until there are calm waters again, until there is peace again, will we be able to see what truly lies before us. When the storm passes by (and it always does), and the winds calm down (and they always do), we will once again see God's "trees of life" stand tall by the shores of our lives.

When Jesus walked upon that stormy sea, He did not fall or waver. He stood up straight and tall, walking, moving forward because He had that peace within Himself. He was that peace. It was as much a part of Him as His feet that literally touched and subdued the cresting waves.

When Peter tried to walk on the water with Christ, he was fine as long as he looked into Jesus' eyes, into that peace Jesus had. However, we know that when Peter began to look at the sea and the storm around him, he lost that peace and spiritual buoyancy that kept him afloat, and Jesus had to rescue him from drowning.

In 1 Corinthians 13:12 (NIV) the apostle Paul said, "For now we see only a reflection as in a mirror," and so do we. Even with all that God graciously reveals to us, we have a somewhat blurred vision of what is and what is yet to be. One day we shall see it as it truly is.

Christ stands firmly on any surface. Whether it is on a rocky shoreline or on the troubled waters of a stormy sea, He never loses His footing. And neither shall we, if we look to the truth and not the world's reflection of the truth.

If a storm does come (and they occasionally do), He will calm the sea as before. When the storm passes and the fog lifts, God will be standing on the shoreline with open arms, welcoming us home.

One more thing I would like to add before I close on this thought. Awhile back after a church meeting, a lady came up to me and gave me a gift, wrapped in a small bag. In it was a crystal prism. She told me a story about how she got this prism, and I think it fits very well with this chapter.

She told me she had recently bought a new frame for one of her pictures, and as she hung it on the wall, the light from one of the windows in her home hit the corner of the frame and gave off a colorful array of prism light. She said it hit the frame just right and a beautiful rainbow of color was cast upon the wall behind it.

As she sat alone looking at the light in her house, she got a word from the Lord regarding this. She felt like the Lord was telling her that just as this array of color cast its reflection all over her house, the Spirit of God was all around her as well.

Prisms (in any form) grab the light around and simply divide that light into a spectrum of separate colors. The light and the colors within that light are always around us. However, it is through the use of prisms that we can see the full spectrum of those colors that are normally hidden from view. It's the same with God. He is always around us. Sometimes, we hear Him within our spirits, and sometimes we may not. Either way, He is with us always.

She reached into the small bag, pulled out one small crystal prism, and said, "Here, I bought two of them, and I wanted you to have one as a reminder of the story I just shared. May you always remember that God is always there each time you see the rainbow from the prism."

I have it hanging in my office. Yes, I do think of her story each time I look at it and remember that God is ever present. Whether we physically see Him, emotionally feel Him or not, He is there with us always in full, living color!

THE INVITATION
Revelation 19:9

RAINBOWS AND REFLECTIONS

The Invitation

You are invited to come dine with me,
from now through all eternity.
Believe in the Father, Son and Holy Ghost,
and dine with Jesus as your host.
To live in heaven eternally,
all you must do is
R.S.V.P.

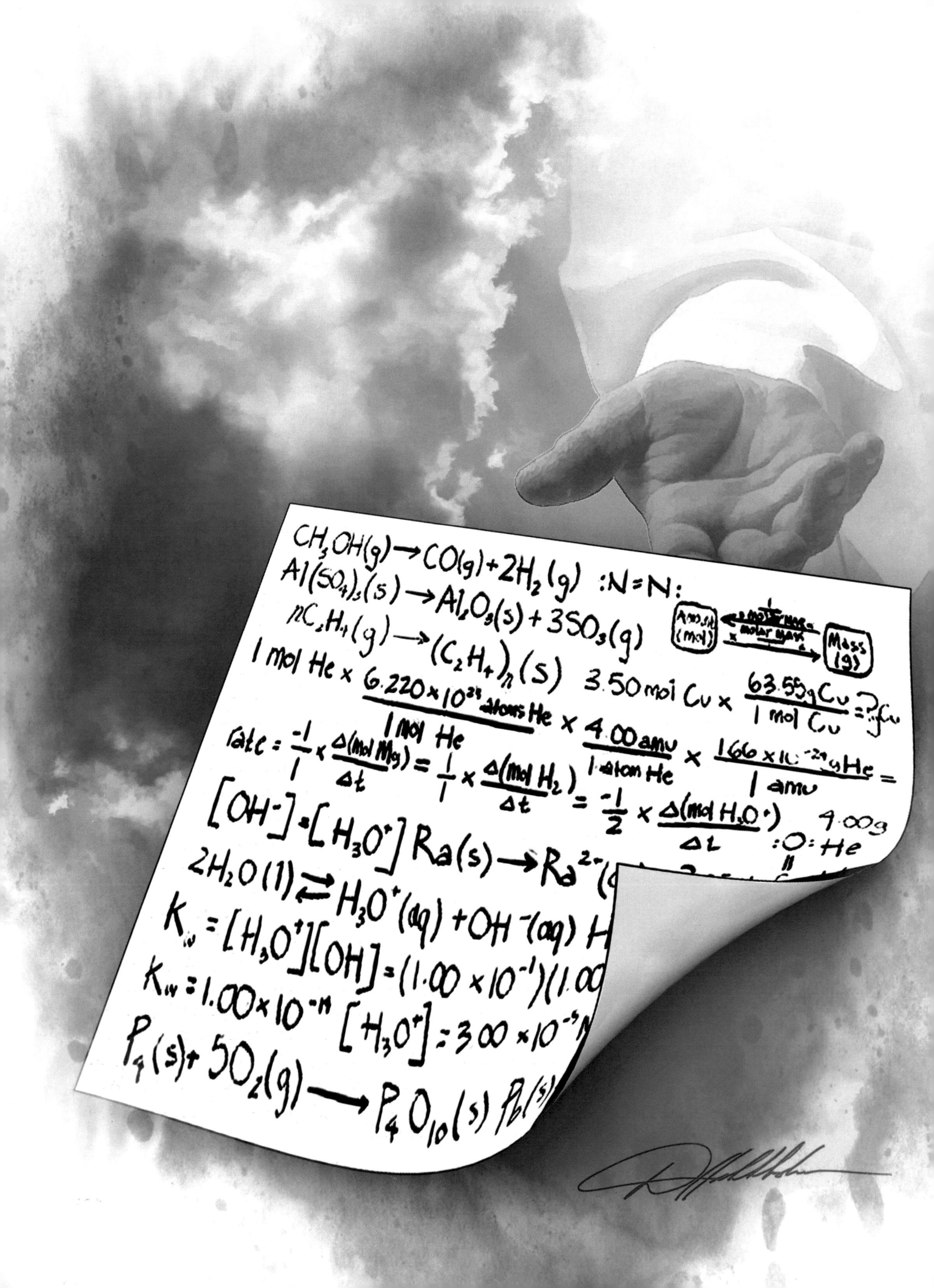

CH3OH(g) → CO(g) + 2H2(g)
:N≡N:
Al(SO4)3(s) → Al2O3(s) + 3SO3(g)
nC2H4(g) → (C2H4)n(s)
Amount (mol)
Mass (g)
3.50 mol Cu × 63.55 g Cu / 1 mol Cu = ? g Cu
1 mol He × 6.220 × 10^23 atoms He / 1 mol He × 4.00 amu / 1 atom He × 1.66 × 10^-24 g He / 1 amu =
4.00 g
[OH-] = [H3O+]
Ra(s) →
2H2O(l) ⇄ H3O+(aq) + OH-(aq)
Kw = [H3O+][OH]
Kw = 1.00 × 10^-14
[H3O+] = 3.00 × 10^-5
P4(s) + 5O2(g) → P4O10(s)

EQUATIONS

Personal Tutoring *of Life*

While in my God Room one morning I began pondering a question my son asked me a couple of days prior, "Why do bad things happen to good people if God is in charge of everything?"

I began to ask God for His wisdom so I could answer correctly as He would have me to do. The Lord answered that request in a most unusual way, a revelation, if you will. I know the word revelation has been misused or overused numerous times, even by me, but in this instance, I think it truly is the correct terminology.

God's answer came as a visual flash, a visualization of a complex mathematical equation on a blackboard. Stunned and bewildered for a moment, I asked, "Lord, I don't even know what this is . . . an equation of some sorts? I don't know these types of equations."

After a slight pause, I heard God whisper, "Exactly."

Now totally confused, I asked God to please explain, because I didn't understand His answer nor would I be able to solve the equation that flashed before me. I am no rocket scientist; I can barely figure out my taxes at the end of the year. His answer was just as simple as the equation was complex.

He explained to me, "That the answer to

> **EQUATIONS**
> Isaiah 55:8

the question I had asked is not found in any scientific equation, nor does man have a rational and correct answer. I showed you that equation simply as an illustration so you might understand my answer in a more definitive way."

The question posed is a complex one, just as the equation (in the world) would also be very complicated to work through and understand.

For a moment let's say you needed to solve the equation placed before you. In that case, you would need to know quantum physics, but first you would need to know trigonometry. Before that, geometry, before that, algebra, and it would chain on down to understanding basic math. Essentially, you need to understand basic math and apply those principles upward, until you would be able to solve more complex equations: $1+1=2$, $2+2=4$, $4+4=8$ and so on.

Next, a full understanding of division and multiplication would be necessary. However, if you did not believe or accept that $2+2=4$ you could not move forward in mathematics. You need to know, understand, apply, and accept the basic principles before you can understand the complex ones.

The same is true in spiritual questions and answers. First we must master basic spiritual concepts, before understanding the more complex questions such as, "Why are bad things allowed to happen to good people?"

So what then are the basics of spiritual understanding?

1. There is a God, one God.
   (see Deuteronomy 6:4).
2. God is a righteous judge.
   (see Psalms 50:6).
3. God is a God of love and He is jealous.
   (see 1 John 4:16 and Deuteronomy 4:24).
4. God is not a respecter of persons, the rain falls on the just as well as the unjust. (see Acts 10:34).

One of the wisest men ever was Solomon, and in Proverbs he stated that the beginning of all wisdom is the fear (respect) of God (see 1:7). Once we understand these basics, then we can begin to grow in our spiritual understanding by solving and understanding the more complex spiritual questions before us. Until then, we simply cannot acquire the answers to those questions because of a lack of spiritual knowledge.

So what then is the answer to why God allows bad things to happen? Rather than making this message a long, twenty-six page document, let me jump from basic math to geometry. In the words of Gerald Mann, an old-time favorite pastor of mine, "It is not what happens that matters, but what happens to what happens that counts."

Let's say, for example, you have lived a good Christian life and been an upright individual. Yet, one evening you find that your house was robbed of all its contents. You had set the alarm in precaution, yet it was bypassed. You may have even prayed over the house before you left and did all you could, but this bad thing happened, and now you are left out in the cold. You are distraught because, in your mind, a bad thing happened to a good person. Why?

God sees it from a slightly different perspective. Let's say, a robbery happened to you (that is what happened), but now let's see how you handle it (what happens to what happens). Will you fall to your knees or shake a fist in anger? Will you simply regroup, collect your thoughts, and try to make the best of what you have left? Or will you hold a grudge toward people, neighborhoods, or even God, thinking that He should have protected you since you prayed over everything before you left?

So was all this simply a test? Perhaps, but if it were a test, then it becomes important in the stand we take. God does care, but He cares far more about your character than the things you had in the house.

By successfully passing the test, we become more grounded in our faith, closer to God, and more mature children of God in the process. You might even say hard times are allowed to give us an opportunity for spiritual promotion. None of us welcome or desire hardships, me included. In fact, we spend most of our lives trying to prevent them, but when calamity strikes, how do we respond? What happens (in us) to what happens?

Remember this if you remember nothing else: We are only here for a short time, but we will live in heaven eternally. If you look at it from that perspective (God's perspective), you will agree that it is not what happens that really matters but what happens to what happens that counts the most. Passing these tests will either add to or subtract from our spiritual character. And when all is said and done, that is all we will have when we enter the pearly gates. We can only take the spiritual treasures with us.

WINGS OF FAITH
poem by Clay Harrison

EQUATIONS OF LIFE

Basically, if you want to know and understand life's complex questions and get the answers right, then hit the books, or in this case, "The Book!" God has given us all the answers in His Word. We just have to start reading more of it, and if we have problems in understanding parts, He has also sent us a private tutor, the Holy Spirit.

The best part about God's Book is that no matter how many times you read it, it is still filled with surprises and hidden messages for you to uncover. Fortunately, unlike many books of today, there are no alternative endings. God always wins in the end, and we get to live happily ever after. Praise be to the Lord!

Wings of Faith

May the wings of faith uphold you
When your cross is hard to bear,
As temptations surround you,
And no one seems to care.

May the wings of faith surround you
And shield you from the pain
When sorrows overcome you
And teardrops fall like rain.

May you know that God is with you
In times of deep despair.
May the spirit, who's within you,
Confirm that He is there!

May the valley of the shadow
Provide angels unaware...
May the wings of faith uphold you
When your cross is hard to bear.

Poet, Clay Harrison

EQUATIONS OF LIFE

Personal Tutoring

The secret to the God Room is simple; yet, much like the Lord Himself, it is also quite complex. When asked by Moses, "Whom shall I say sent me?" The Lord answered, "I AM." This is the simplest of answers, yet it is deep when analyzed closely.

The basis of the God Room is not that it is a specific place (though it can be) but rather, any place or space where we spend quality time alone with God. Sometimes we simply share time together looking into the beauty the Lord has provided for us. Other times, we converse and spend time talking about things, but remember that in any conversation, one must listen as well as speak. Listening is perhaps the biggest key to the God Room. Let me explain why.

Many, if not most of the visions I have received from the Lord regarding the paintings I have created have come to me around two o'clock in the morning. I have been awakened in the middle of the night for years with visions, or ideas I felt the Lord laid on my heart. As a matter of fact, I have a large board with erasable markers set close by, just because this has happened so often. I get the idea, get up and scribble the details on the board, and then crawl back in bed. This is almost a standard routine as the

ABOVE THE MANTEL
1 Corinthians 2:9

occasion arises.

One evening a number of years ago, I was once again awakened at 2:30 a.m. I got up, wrote the details of the vision on the board, and crawled back into bed. As I was drifting off to sleep, I told the Lord, "Lord, I don't mind getting up doing this for You. I am privileged and honored to be Your servant. However, Lord, can't You give me these visions during the day during normal hours? I would just as gladly do them."

The Lord almost immediately said (and I am paraphrasing here of course): "It is the only time you shut up and I can get a word in edgewise" (not the exact words, but to that effect).

From that time, I began listening in my God Room time with the Lord. Many times we spend time in prayer with God, talking to Him about what we need or what others may need in our prayers. Then we get up and continue on with our day when God is saying, "Hey! What about Me? Don't I get a chance to respond here?"

How can we get a word from the Lord or hear God if we don't take the time to "wait upon the Lord"? (see Isaiah 40:31). I know it sounds like a "duh" question, but we all have a tendency to do that. Now, I take time to just sit and wait. It's hard to do these days, since we are all part of such a hustle-bustle society, but it is a must. I want to hear what God has to say, and if I am not quiet and wait, I will probably miss whatever He has for me at that time. It was a lesson that took a number of years for me to learn, but a lesson well learned in the end.

Once again, I was awakened in the middle of the night by the Lord, but this time He wanted to show me something quite special in the form of a vision. I had a short dream prior to this concerning the salvation of my three sons, when the Lord began to console me by taking me on a small tour (vision if you will). This journey of sorts in my mind's eye took place in heaven. It did not involve passing down the golden streets or floating above the clouds. Rather, the setting was in a mansion, my mansion that God has prepared for me.

God reminded me of the Bible passage that reveals "Only what is done for Christ shall last" (see 1 Corinthians. 3:9-13). Everything we have done here on earth shall be put to the test of fire. Those that were done for Christ shall remain, and all else shall be burned in the fire.

As we strolled around the mansion God prepared for me, I could see all of my paintings hanging on huge walls that stretched so high I can't even estimate the dimensions. Each painting did not seem to be exactly as I had painted it. They were not painted at all but were some sort of golden embossment of those paintings. Each shone brightly as a token of great worth. I noticed other items around the house on tables, pillars, and stands, each signifying a deed or something I had done for the glory of God.

These were all my spiritual possessions, my treasures stored up in heaven, things that would never tarnish or be taken from me for all eternity. These were things I had done for the glory of God, but much more than that was the house itself. The mansion I was to dwell in all the days of my eternal life was actually a standing, living representation of who I was in Christ.

As I walked around each room, I noticed it was filled with tokens, or reminders. It was like walking around inside the life I lived when I was on earth, a full representation of who I was in the Lord.

I began to realize that when we walk into someone's mansion in heaven, it will be like walking inside that saint of God and seeing who they are rather than where they live. All he or she ever did for the Lord while here on earth will be inside the mansion in plain view. I realized that, yes, we can take it with us, but only those things done for God's sake, not our earthly earnings or achievements. It was odd because although all these items were not presented as trophies of which to be proud, but rather, humble affirmations of the life I had lived for Christ.

There were sincere achievements for the glory of God in each mansion, but no expressions of a grandiose nature for the glory of man. Indeed no one could say, "I got this because I did so and so," because if it were not for the grace and power of God, none of these things would have come to pass in the first place. Perhaps "tokens of obedience" would best describe the artifacts there. Everything had a shine to it like highly polished bronze or silver, and their glow lit up the entire house.

Then God walked me to the center of the house where a huge mantel stood, a glorious mantel of shining gold and silver. On the mantel were similar tokens, but these were somewhat different in that they actually shone from within, as if illuminated by a candle or a flame, though they contained no fiery substance that I could see. They shone brightly with a soft diffusion, and the light never

TIME IS AT HAND
Matthew 24:30

dimmed but radiated throughout the entire house, a perfect blend of visual harmony.

On the wall above the mantel was a huge mirror not like any I had seen before. This mirror had depth, great depth. It was as if when you looked into it, you could see through it at the same time. In this mirror were also similar lighted objects that were on the mantel but many, many more lights. Some were close up, and some were off in the distance, as far as my eyes could see. God explained that these signified the souls I had won to the Lord, either directly or indirectly through my life's work while on earth. It was so captivating, I could not take my eyes off of it.

Daniel 12:3 NIV
"Those who are wise will shine like the brightness of the heavens, and those who lead many to righteousness, like the stars for ever and ever."

Then God directed my sight back to the mantel where the main objects were placed. He said they were the most valuable possessions of all. These represented the saved souls of my children.

The saved souls of my children! I broke down in tears and fell to the ground, praising and worshiping the Lord for His goodness and mercy.

Those who have saved children have

ABOVE THE MANTEL

the most prized possession one could ever acquire, here or in heaven. Never feel short-changed in life, no matter what your situation is, as long as your children know the Lord. You could never ask for anything more than knowing your children will be with you forever in paradise. We all realize this, but having a visual representation seemed to bring the message home even more.

Jesus said when He left here that He was going to prepare a place for us, that God Himself has many mansions, one for each of us. We shall have those glorious mansions shining brightly forever, mansions with wonderful and glorious things placed throughout them, including a central mantel. The glory of the home itself is a testimony to all we have done for the Lord through obedience to Him and for His name's sake. In essence, the Lord shall provide our mansions in heaven, but we will decorate it with what we have done for Him while down here.

We know not the things God has prepared for us, both for His glory and for our comfort and enjoyment. And if you have loved ones who are saved, they shall forever shine brightly, warming your heavenly mansion for all eternity. These are keepsakes of a loving God whose grace has made it all possible and who desires to share that glory and joy with you now and forever.

The life we live here counts for so much more then we can possibly imagine, and these testaments and affirmations of that life with its struggles, hardships, and sacrifices are worth it all. Oh, if you could have only seen!

It makes one wonder if so many young mothers could only realize what they are truly giving up when they decide to abort a young child before birth. If they could have seen what the Lord showed me that night, they would know that they are not only robbing that child, but also robbing themselves. Those lights on the mantel made the home in heaven what it was, warming and lighting the entire house like steadfast beacons shining forth the declaration, "These are standing testaments for the Lord's glory!"

I never got the chance or opportunity to look down the street, but I could only imagine seeing other houses shining like Christmas every day, with glowing lights coming from within the houses instead of on the rooftops.

Indeed, there is no need for street lighting in heaven, for all that is of Christ shall emit its own light, that glorious light of God. God will also place on our hearts all the wonderful callings we share together as one body, one community, one love, the love to serve the Lord.

Take heart, my brothers and sisters in the Lord, during troublesome times and always remember your home in heaven awaits you. You are building your own residence yourself with each act of kindness, giving of yourself to lead some soul to the Lord. You are erecting your own eternal dwelling place daily and the glorious mantel that will be its centerpiece.

Now is the time to store up those treasures in heaven. As the words spoken by C.T. Studd in the late 1800's declare:

"Only one life, 'twill soon be past,
Only what's done for Christ will last!"

HOME AT LAST
Matthew 25:23

BEHOLD HE COMES
Matthew 24:30

DANNY HAHLBOHM
at print signing convention

Danny Hahlbohm was born in Mineola, New York on June of 1949. He grew up on the eastern end of Long Island, New York until 1968 when he enlisted in the Armed Forces and was sent overseas. Honorably Discharged in 1972 Danny began painting for galleries and auctions houses across the nation.

Two years later he started touring the country, promoting himself and exhibiting his work nationally from coast to coast. Danny was approached by one of the largest publishers in the art field while on tour in 1978, and they began distributing reproductions of his works throughout the country.

Within a year Danny released "Footprints in the Sand." This resulted in world recognition, putting the art work of Danny Hahlbohm into the homes of millions of people. In his forty year career there have been over 100 different prints of Danny's paintings reproduced and distributed to over thirty countries around the world.

Danny's style and technique have brought him much recognition, ranging from billboards of his work, to magazine covers, CD covers, headstones in cemeteries, limited edition plates and puzzles. He was even honored for openings in select theaters in Texas for Mel Gibson's "The Passion of the Christ." Although Danny never took any art lessons, he has developed his style to such a simple method of application, that he has taught many art classes throughout the United States. These art classes are currently available through Danny's website at www.inspired-art.com.

Danny's works have been hung in some of the most prestigious galleries across the nation:
New Bedford Whaling Museum in New Bedford, Massachusetts
Swanson Gallery in San Francisco, California
Corner Stone Gallery in Dublin, Ireland
Americana Gallery in Carmel, California
5th Avenue Studio Gallery in Mount Dora, Florida

Among some of his collectors are:
Benny Hinn
Jim MacInnes (one of the principle leaders in "The Jesus Movement" 1972)
Captain Burke (owner of Windjammer Cruises)
Joyce Meyers (Danny did her portrait in 2001)
Rod Parsley (Danny did his portrait in 2009)

For more information on the artwork of Danny Hahlbohm
please go to his website at:

www.inspired-art.com

All of Danny's paintings can be seen on his website.
You can purchase any one of these magnificent pieces
of art to put into your home or office
and they make wonderful gifts in blessing others as well.

If you wish to contact Danny Hahlbohm regarding this book
or his artwork you may do so at his email address:

inspired-art@comcast.net

THE GOD ROOM

For more information on the the God Room by Danny Hahlbohm
please go to his God Room website at:

www.godroom.net

Danny and Diana Hahlbohm also have a worldwide
network TV broadcast of the God Room.
These broadcasts are seen in many countries around the world
bringing inspiration and comfort to those who have watched them.

If you wish to contact Danny Hahlbohm regarding
these broadcasts you may do so at:

inspiredart@icloud.com

List of ILLUSTRATIONS

THE GOD ROOM

THE GOD ROOM

I was reluctant to do this painting at first because thought it was too dark and would not sell well. However the Lord told me to do it. He was more interested in getting the message out than sales. He was right.

This is another painting I was reluctant to do, but it ended up saving a young girl's life. Praise be to God! His love is never-ending.

While in deep prayer one day I felt the Lord put His hand under my chin and He whispered ever so gently, "Seek My face child, not just My hand." So I had to do a painting on that experience, However I used one of my models instead of myself for this piece.

The Lord gave me a vision of the Holy Spirit decending with His robe fluttered after Him, almost like a dove's wings.

This painting was influenced by my sunset experience that I shared on page 35. Reflecting on all Christ had done for me while on a Florida beach one day, this vision came to me so I painted it. However, this time with humility.

Roses are the world's way of expressing love. The Holy Spirit and the blood of Christ is God's way of showing His love. I wanted to incorporate the two Ideas together to create this painting. This is my wife's favorite piece.

My cousin Gary posed for Santa in this painting. Wearing a Santa outfit in Florida is not a lot of fun. The painting, however, came out as I hoped it would, giving honor, glory and homage to Christ Jesus on His day.

We all make up the "body of Christ." Obviously, I could not depict every type of profession to signify this, but I included as many as I could. Like the old saying, "You may be the only Jesus that some people ever see." It is a great resonsibility being the King's embassador..

THE GOD ROOM

This painting is also one of my favorites because it represents the wonderful and mighty wisdom the Lord has in the game of life. He has made His move by giving us His Son; now, it is our move. Will we accept Him or not?

I did this piece simply to depict that famous well-known parable Jesus talked about in His celebrated "Sermon on the Mount."

What a glorious day! The birth of our King, the Savior of the world. If Christ had never come, we all would be lost. I used two of our church members to model for this piece. Unknown to all of us, including them, she was pregnant when the picture was taken.

I did this painting not to present myself but to show where my inspiration for painting comes from. I look up for His divine inspiration. I can only hope others will view it in the same light.

We Christians are at war, a spiritual war that requires the right armor for our defence and protection.

There is no greater weapon that we have in the "Christian arsenal" than prayer and intercession. And there are no greater prayers uttered than a mother's prayers for her children. I know this to be true in my own life.

As Christians, we have two birthdays. One birth leads to death; the other leads to life. One is of the flesh and will return to the dust; the other shall live in a heavenly realm forever.

We serve a mighty and glorious King. A King whose Kingdom is one of love, compassion and grace. This kingdom shall never fall and the King, our king, will reign forever.

We sometimes wish the Lord would come quickly because we long to be with Him. No one wants this reunion more than Christ Himself, but there are still those who need to be saved. So the King awaits.

THE GOD ROOM

THE GOD ROOM

Interesting story, my publisher wanted me to do my personal rendition of "The Last Supper" painting since "Footprints In The Sand" was selling so well. However, I told her I could not do the piece because I did not feel inspired by God to do it. She hired another artist to complete the painting she wanted. That new piece failed miserably. Later that year the Lord spoke to me and said it was a test for me, to see if money meant more then His inspiration or obedience to Him. The Lord then inspired me to do a similar piece ("The Invitation") and to date it is still one of my best sellers ever. I painted and released this piece in 1980.

This is a fairly good representation of the vision I received from God when I asked Him, "What is the meaning of life?"

It is the poem by Clay Harrision that makes this piece. My simple illustration was only meant to accent his words. I thank Mr. Harrison for permission to use this poem.

This is the vision of my mantel the Lord showed me when He took me on a journey to Heaven to see the mansion He prepared for me.

Yes indeed, the time is at hand. Look around, not with your natural eyes, but with your spiritual eyes. Paul said the end will be near when people become lovers of themselves more than lovers of God.

The original version of this painting was created in 1983 as "Welcome Home." It was never meant to be sold or reproduced. It is my #1 favorite piece I have ever painted.

One day Jesus will return as King and claim back all that is His. I used many of my church members as models for this including my Pastor Jim MacInnes who is on a horse alongside Jesus Himself at His return.

I created this logo for my local church. Lifting up Jesus is what we do. All honor and glory belong to Him alone. Amen.